I Thirst

Seven Trips to India

by Michael de Jong

Canadian Cataloguing in Publication Data
De Jong, Michael Douglas, 1936–
I thirst
ISBN 0-9683566-0-5
1. De Jong, Michael Douglas, 1936– --Journeys--India.
2. Spiritual biography. 3. India--Description and travel.
I. Title.
BL73.D4A3 1998   291.4'092   C98-910345-5

Produced by: Peanut Butter Publishing
Editor: Suzanne Bastedo
Text Design: Fiona Raven
Cover Design: Gordon Finlay

First printing June 1998

FOCUS PRESS
P.O. Box 47022
Denman Place P.O.
Vancouver, British Columbia
Canada V6G 3E1
email: IThirst@bc.sympatico.ca
Telephone: (604) 816-8401

Printed in Canada

~

Dedication

To my daughters,
Maureen, Diane and Carolyn,
who are my joy and inspiration

Table of Contents

~

Preface

This book is the story of my thirst for peace, harmony, and adventure and how it has led me to India seven times in the last seven years. I feel privileged to have been able to travel, and want to share my experiences with others, especially my children and grandchildren.

My journey to recovery began in 1991. The first section of the book describes how I started on that journey, which launched me to India and to transforming my life. The following sections present stories about my seven trips to India, ranging from looking for miracle-workers and working with Mother Teresa to the joys of experiencing India itself. Along the way, I visited ashrams, went on retreats, tried to learn to meditate, and met a number of gurus. Although I travelled throughout India, my primary focus was Calcutta, the headquarters of Mother Teresa and the Missionaries of Charity, the organization she founded to work with the sick, the dying and the poor.

For the early years of my work with the Missionaries of Charity, I managed to avoid the death part of the job. One year, however, I was asked to help clean up a body, wrap it in a shroud and deliver it to the burning place. By the following year, I was working as an undertaker. During my last two trips to India, my primary interest was in the medical field. A bit squeamish at first, I became fascinated with the procedures in an operating theatre. Recently, after two years of working and living in a leprosy community where most of the operations were amputations, I have sought a broader experience and volunteered to go travelling with some of the doctors doing medical camps.

The title of this book was partly inspired by Mother Teresa. In the houses where Mother Teresa and the Missionaries of Charity cared for the sick and the poor, there were many crucifixes. On each was a little sign, I Thirst, which reflected their mission statement: "to relieve the thirst of Christ by serving the poor." Mother Teresa and her organization inspired me to learn to love and care in a way I had not thought possible for me, a hard-nosed business type with a thirst for alcohol and power. Working and living with other volunteers and the sisters changed my perspective on life, and started a journey which brought my life renewed purpose.

∾

Many of the names and circumstances in this book have been changed for obvious reasons. Some details may have become obscure in my memory, but the experiences I describe actually happened.

~

Introduction

Whenever I drive through the countryside and watch the fields flow by, a certain peace descends on me, bringing me back to my roots in Holland. I was the fourth child of a family of eight sisters and three brothers, all except one born in Holland (one sister was born in Canada). It was my good fortune to have spent my first twelve years in the province of Friesland, in the village of Stiens. It was the most tranquil time of my life. I was carefree, roaming the sugar beet and potato fields, jumping ditches, and watching the boat traffic in the canals. In the winter, skating from village to village was my favourite activity. Every spring we searched for duck eggs, a wonderful delicacy. I became obsessive about looking for them, and often found more than anyone else.

In Friesland, the language is different from the rest of Holland, and the inhabitants are different as well. We tend to be stubborn and arrogant. We are also competitive and have an overwhelming passion to be truthful. Our motto could be: "My word is my bond."

I do not know why my family emigrated to Canada, but I do know that marked a major shift in my life. Like many immigrants, we had to learn a new language and culture, and were all affected in different ways. My father, for instance, had been self-employed and reasonably secure in Holland. In the new country, he had none of these benefits. His personality changed, and with it, our lives changed too.

My father became driven to be successful. Money became his main goal in life and we children were recruited to add to the family treasure chest. My first contributions were the proceeds from my paper route. All the other paper boys had money to spend on the latest clothing fads, as well as plenty of money for pop and candy. I had none, and it was one of my major resentments. We were a family where piety and religious obedience were foremost. Our parents were tough taskmasters, also skilled manipulators and controllers. My father had a vicious temper and lived by the credo: "Spare the rod and spoil the child." Often he would defend his actions as being the will of God. My siblings and I were rarely praised, often scolded. The rivalry between us was intense. Today, all of us in our own ways are dealing with the pain of our upbringing. I know that my emotional scars run deep.

I married at the age of twenty-one, only to carry on the family tradition of emotional and physical abuse with my spouse and children. Today I shudder at my role. I was horrid. We had been married for thirty years when my wife finally escaped to freedom.

The first four years of my single life were dreadful. My inflated ego was devastated by my wife's leaving. I sought comfort in riotous living, as well as sex and alcohol. Nothing worked. After five years, I hit bottom and started to scratch and crawl my way out of the hole I was in. My journey to recovery began then and continues today.

After more than sixty years on this planet, I have concluded that I can be much more than the product of my environment. I believe that I create my own experience, and I have finally created a life I find worth living. The path to discovery and recovery, although bumpy from time to time, is opening up for me. It has led me to some amazing places, both geographically and emotionally. Geographically, I have travelled within Canada and the United States, and have made many trips to Europe as well as Asia, India, Australia, New Zealand, the Caribbean, South America, and Africa. Emotionally, my thirst for alcohol has turned into a thirst for a new life of peace and harmony. I have committed myself to learning humility, which feels quite awkward for a boastful and arrogant Dutchman.

Yet the Dutch traits of determination and persistence keep serving me well. Today I experience an abundance of tranquillity and serenity and enjoy relationships that work, including with my children and grandchildren. Unfortunately, my former wife and I have not yet been able to establish a relationship with each other in our new lifestyles. One of my major challenges has been to forgive myself for the role I played in the relationship with her, and to give up both my guilt and my resentment towards her for the role she played.

During the period when I was particularly struggling, I attended a course which dealt with forgiveness. I bought audio tapes and went to a workshop and read books on forgiveness, but even then I resisted. I was so sure that I was right to feel angry and rejected, and said so until someone asked me one day: "What would you rather be

— right or happy?" "Of course I would rather be happy," I said, "but . . ." The minute I said "but," I realized that (yet again) I needed to surrender my need to be right. When I did let go, a burden was lifted from my shoulders. The feeling of freedom was similar to that of my youth when I could explore the fields and jump ditches in a carefree manner.

I keep experiencing bumps like that on the way to peace and harmony. But one thing I know is how to persevere. The peace and harmony which looked so inaccessible at other times in my life no longer loom in the distance. They are now within my reach.

Section
1

≈

Journey to Recovery

Chapter 1

∼

Cap'n Crunch

During the thirty years of my marriage, I mostly did what I thought was expected of me, which was to provide materially for my family. I made a poor employee — I needed to be in control, and if I wasn't, I changed jobs. I changed jobs often. Then, for fifteen years, my wife and I ran our own business, and we succeeded well at that. Success was not enough for me to be content, however; I always thirsted for something more without being aware of what that something was. This thirst led me into many jobs and adventures, from driving a truck to applying bandages to utility poles. Those experiences seem far removed from my current thirst for peace and harmony, and I don't want to dwell on them. At the same time, I don't want to shrink from looking at my life before I was aware of spiritual needs — mine or those of others. Then, as now, I was easily bored with doing the same old things. Because I loved adventure, I developed fanciful notions and craved new challenges. The following story is about one of those cravings. While the story is humorous, I know today that it was as much fuelled by my taste for rum as by my thirst for adventure.

∼

In the 1960s, I was operating a thriving insurance business in British Columbia's Lower Mainland, but that wasn't enough to keep me occupied. I used to sit by the Fraser River and daydream and watch the boats go by. I would visualize large freighters crossing oceans, plowing through waves as large as a house, and arriving in many exotic places. I visualized myself meandering through the great ports of the world. Then reality would set in and remind me that I had responsibilities.

As I daydreamed, I watched a steady procession of commercial fishboats plying their way up and down the river. Going down river, the boats rode high in the water as they headed for the fishing grounds. Coming back, many were so loaded with their yield of fish that their hulls almost disappeared in the water. To me, the skippers of the boats looked content as they passed to and fro. I was certain they were reaping huge financial rewards since I thought that the price of salmon was almost criminal. One day, I decided to participate in this lucrative enterprise.

First, I sought out the fishermen who were mending nets and repairing their craft, to see who would sell me a boat. All complained about how poor the catch was and how the cost of doing business had made fishing unprofitable, yet none would sell their boats. I was puzzled. If things were so bad, why they wouldn't sell their boats? A friend explained that people who fished for a living were like farmers. "They're always complaining," he said. That made sense to me since my farmer brother-in-law had never admitted to having a good crop. Yet each year he bought a piece of expensive new equipment, paid cash for his new house, and seemed to have plenty of money for vacations.

Having decided that the fishermen had probably made a pact to limit competition, I was more than ever determined to get involved in the fishing industry. Finally, someone told me that Gary, the owner of the vessel *Cheryll-Ann,* might want to sell. Gary was trying to work full-time and fish part-time, and his employer had given him an ultimatum: quit fishing or lose your job. Since I was self-employed, no one could give me such an ultimatum, so we struck a deal at $20,000. I could hardly believe my good fortune in acquiring this fine-looking vessel so cheap! The price even included nets and government permits. Permission to fish was generally limited to a twenty-four-hour period once a week, mostly from 8:00 a.m. Monday to 8:00 a.m. Tuesday. Gary promised to show me the ropes and teach me how to fish. The following Monday, we fished for eighteen hours before Gary called it a day. He had shown me all there was to know to be successful, he said. It seemed very, very simple to me.

I had to wait a whole week before an another opening for fishing was granted. My son-in-law, Karl, volunteered to be my deck-hand. The docks were a beehive of activity at six in the morning, although the opening wasn't scheduled until eight. The skipper of the boat next to us advised us to get to the fishing ground early to get a good spot. I untied the boat and gave it shove. As it was gliding away from the dock, I jumped on board and pushed the throttle gently forward. The boat responded and we joined the fleet heading out into the river. We were one of about fifteen hundred boats. I was thrilled, and convinced that I was about to make my fortune.

Soon the boats were lined up about ten feet apart along the bank of the river. I joined the queue and waited for the radio signal from the fisheries patrol boat. While waiting, I was busy congratulating myself on how easy this was, and discussing with Karl our strategy. We were going to release our net and scoop up our fortune. Karl was going to drive the boat to the other side of the river — a distance of about five hundred feet — while I released the net from the stern. When the fisheries patrol boat gave the order to start fishing, all fifteen hundred boats roared their engines, each vying to be the first to reach the other side where the unsuspecting salmon were trying to swim upstream. Karl decided to be cautious and go more slowly than the other boats while I was letting the gill net gently off the reel (called a "drum").

We had gone about fifty feet from shore when I noticed that on our left side we were parked on top of the net of our neighbour, who at the same time noticed our transgression. He stood on his stern waving his arms furiously and shouting obscenities.

"We better turn right and get off this guy's net," I shouted to Karl.

"Ay, ay, captain," he responded sarcastically, then turned the wheel to the right while I tried to untangle my net from the neighbour's. We hadn't travelled twenty feet when I noticed that now our boat was parked on top of the net to the right of us, and *that* skipper was now yelling threats at us. Suddenly he disappeared into the cabin of his boat. When he returned, he was popping a shotgun shell into the chamber of a gun. As he aimed the gun in our direction, I asked him not to shoot and promised we would leave and go somewhere else. With a great deal of difficulty, we recovered our net and moved away.

By then, the current of the river had increased in velocity due to the changing tide. The *Cheryll-Ann* had three stations from which to manoeuvre: one in front in the cabin, one just behind the cabin mid-ship, and one at the stern. Karl had sufficiently recovered from our trials to make coffee on the oil stove. I, too, had regained my composure, and was at the rear station, navigating us to friendlier territory, when I looked up and noticed smoke pouring from the roof of the cabin. Next I saw a stove pipe hurtling out of the window and smoke billowing from the door and windows. I rushed into the cabin to assist in fighting the fire.

As we tried to do something about the cabin fire, I noticed that we were moving even faster with the current and were getting dangerously close to the rocky shore. We were getting closer and closer to shore and I feared we would puncture our plywood hull on the rocks. I clambered onto the bow of the boat to drop the anchor, then rejoined Karl in fighting the fire. After a few minutes, Karl wondered aloud why the shore seemed even closer, and we soon had our answer. As I looked over at the bow, the last of the anchor rope disappeared over the side. The rope had not been tied to the cleat — and now the anchor was gone. With a steel pole, I managed to keep our vessel pushed off the rocks while Karl managed to douse the fire. Then, with our hurt pride, we chugged up river.

A half-mile later, we came upon a large gap between boats. I decided we should be able to avoid any difficulties here, and proceeded to put the net in the water. For the first hundred yards, things went smoothly. Suddenly part of the net submerged. Another boat pulled alongside and someone yelled over: "You're hung up on a tree on the bottom of the river! You'd better cut your net free!"

Reluctantly I got out my butcher knife and freed the net from the snag. In the first four hours of fishing, we had managed to lose a quarter of our net, half our stove pipe, and our anchor, as well as the anchor chain and rope. And we hadn't caught a single fish.

I decided to return to home port and replace the broken net and make the other repairs. Since the river was affected by the tides of the nearby ocean, the early morning calm had now been replaced by a fast-paced current. We found that approaching the dock was now very difficult. I made about six attempts to dock. As soon as the boat got close, the current would sweep it away again. I decided that the next time we neared the dock, I would jump across with a rope. When we approached within four feet, I jumped. Unfortunately, the rope I was holding was only two feet long. Instead of sensibly letting go, I clung to the rope and fell into the river. Weighed down by my heavy rain gear, I thought I would drown. I hollered at Karl to bring the boat closer, which he did, almost running over me in the process. Somehow I managed to climb onto the dock, then watched Karl trying to negotiate the boat close enough to throw me a longer rope. After a few more failed attempts, we managed to secure the boat to the dock. We spent the rest of the afternoon making repairs.

If I had had common sense, I would have quit for the day and followed the advice of others, who said to seek out someone qualified to fish and have that person teach me all there was to know. But my pig-headed Dutch nature said I could do it, and soon we headed out — this time for the open sea rather than the congested river.

Over the next few hours, we set our net out several times, but still did not catch any fish. After the sun had gone down, we finally hit pay dirt. (I later discovered that the ocean water is not murky like the water of the river, so during daylight hours the fish can see the net and swim around it.) With our first set, we had hundreds of fish. Almost all of them had spun themselves into the net, however, and we spent hours carefully picking them out.

At 2:00 a.m., we were about to retrieve another loaded net when the engine refused to start. After we had worked on our broken engine for two hours, our flashlight batteries stopped working. We continued repairs using our abundant supply of matches for light. At seven, I started to haul in the heavy net by hand since we had only one hour of fishing time left. Our net again produced an abundant crop, including six larger fish. Just before eight, while I was hauling in the net, Karl managed to get the engine started and we set off to the area where a fleet of fish buyers was moored. We managed to dock the *Cheryll-Ann* without incident. Just as we were about to unload, a fishery patrol boat came alongside and asked how many fish we had caught.

"One thousand," I said.

"Congratulations," he replied, "so far you have the largest catch of the fleet."

I was beaming and the fish buyer was pleased that I had come to his boat to sell my catch. Our elation was short-lived. The fish buyer's deck-hand opened all my hatches to transfer our catch to his boat.

"But you have only six fish that we're interested in!" he said. "All the others are garbage fish and no good to us."

Red-faced, we headed for the fuel dock to refill our tanks. I tried several times to bring the boat into the fuel dock when finally the impatient attendant jumped from the dock onto my boat and expertly docked the boat himself. He said the secret to docking was to use lots of power to guide the boat into the dock. I thanked him profusely for this very helpful tip, and we headed home. As we approached our slip, I remembered the attendant's instruction to use the power. When the current started to take hold of the *Cheryll-Ann,* I moved the lever forward to get a little more power. That didn't seem to be enough, so I moved the lever forward a bit more. The boat still didn't respond, so I gave the lever another push. Suddenly the boat lurched forward and into the bow of another boat. In a flash, my hull had a gaping four-foot hole in it. Fortunately, the other boat did not sustain any damage other than a scrape. I had to take some steel wool and erase the blue paint from my boat off the white hull of the other boat.

The loud crash had attracted the attention of many other fishermen, some of whom had witnessed my earlier escapades. One christened me "Cap'n Crunch," a title that stuck with me for my entire career as a commercial fisherman. That was the politest name I was called. When I later talked about our repair jobs at sea, others were horrified to hear that we were using open flame in and around the engine and bilges, where there is usually an accumulation of oils and gasoline. We could have blown ourselves sky high, they said. At the end of the day, we sat down and calculated our finances. Fish sales: $32. Net repair: $150. Fuel: $50. Anchor: $65. Stove repair: $25. Boat repair: $100. Net loss: $338.

~

For two seasons, Cap'n Crunch wreaked havoc on the fishing fleet. Many times, the *Cheryll-Ann* had to be towed into port for numerous mechanical breakdowns. I had a bad habit of getting the fishing net caught in the propeller and thus incapacitating the boat. Since in the middle of the ocean there are no road signs, and I had no training reading other navigational aids, I often got lost. And on two occasions, I had my net in the water in areas closed to fishing, was apprehended by the fisheries patrol vessel, and required to appear in court and pay a fine. The second time, the judge gave me a hefty fine and warned me that the next time, my fishing license would be cancelled. With that stern warning, I admitted defeat and put the *Cheryll-Ann* on the market.

A few weeks later, I received a phone call from a man asking me to bring the boat's papers to his lawyer's office and sign a transfer of ownership in exchange for $29,000 — my asking price. With the proceeds of the sale, I went to the repair shop to settle my final account of $5,500. This left me a profit of $4,500 after two seasons of fishing. A few days after the sale had been completed, I received an urgent phone call from the marina where the *Cheryll-Ann* had been moored. The boat was sinking! The leaks created by two seasons of abuse were starting to deteriorate to the point where the vessel needed almost daily attention. I hadn't bothered to inform the new owner about these and a few other deficiencies in the boat. With great trepidation, I decided to come clean and call the lawyer who had given me the $29,000. He said that he would pass the information to his client. Within a few minutes, I received a call from the new owner who asked if I would tend to the vessel for a few days while he contemplated its future.

"Are you not going to fish her ?" I asked.

"No," he said, "I only wanted the license attached to the boat. I have no interest in the boat itself." I decided to push my luck.

"Can I have the boat?" I asked.

"Let me check with my partner," he answered. The next day, he called again to tell me that as soon as he removed the salmon license from the boat it would automatically receive a ground fish license. This license would probably fetch $1,000, so I could purchase the boat for that amount. I agreed, went back to the lawyer's office, signed the documents and paid the money. On the advice of a friend, I advertised the ground fish license for $1,500. It sold within hours for full price. Then my friend, on behalf of his brother, offered me $1,500 for the *Cheryll-Ann*. I quickly accepted.

I managed to make a small profit even out of that fishing fiasco. Once again, I was fortunate that my thirst for adventure had left me with more memories to treasure than to regret.

This photograph was taken just after my Cap'n Crunch adventure ended.
Since I had failed at fishing, I decided to try my hand at art.
Steveston, British Columbia

Chapter 2

~

The Retreat

Their lives were transformed, they were different, they had seen the light, they had spent twenty-eight days at a retreat near Montreal. Once a month, happy and contented, a new batch of graduates would arrive back at the Vancouver church I attended. Everyone who had been there strongly recommended the retreat experience. They talked about the wonderful changes in their lives and about spiritual renewal. It was 1991, and although my life was starting to improve, I thought I could use some help in getting to understand God. I decided to go to the Montreal retreat, little knowing that my stay there would be a turning point in my life.

What the people back in Vancouver hadn't told me — or I hadn't heard — was that the retreat was actually an addiction treatment centre.

~

The eighty-mile trip from the airport by van was pleasant, and I arrived at an attractive building located beside a snow-covered lake. The place looked like winter wonderland, with everything sparkling with fresh snow and the trees capped with white. Now, I thought, it's *my* turn at happiness.

Soon after I arrived, I realized that I was at a treatment centre for people with problems. As we introduced each other, words like "co-dependency," "control," and "intolerance" filled the reception hall. My first reaction was that I was not too thrilled at having to spend the next twenty-eight days with what must be a bunch of alcoholics, drug addicts, and weirdos. My second reaction was that even though I was there by mistake, the twenty other people that I had just met were sure in need of help. Since I have *my* act together, I thought, I can be of some help to them.

The first few days we spent sharing our aspirations for ourselves and what we wanted to accomplish in the time there. From there we went to a process called "the hot seat" where each of us were questioned by three staff members. The questions were very penetrating, with no holds barred. I wasn't looking forward to my turn, but thought that since I didn't have any problems it should be easy.

It turned out to be anything but easy. I quickly found myself on the defence as Gordon, the director, began questioning every aspect of my life. The whole time he was questioning me, part of my brain was busy thinking about the other people who had been in the hot seat. Now they had *real* problems, I thought. For instance, June. My goodness, what a mess this woman was! An artist, a cook, did every kind of drug, been married three times, a life in total disarray, and she was just in her thirties. I was lucky that I was not like her! Why, why, was Gordon picking on me? I wasn't like June! I wasn't like Albert, either. Albert from Detroit was a gangster type. He'd had three convictions for driving while under the influence. How dare Gordon suggest that I too might have a drinking problem? I had never had a drunk driving charge! And how about big Dave from Montreal who was into hard drugs — and into crime to support his habit? He spent a lot of time in jail. I wasn't like that. Why, why, was Gordon attacking me? I kept saying, "But, but, but . . . I'm not at all like these people!"

After all, I had discovered a great and wonderful church where I had heard about the retreat in Montreal. As someone raised in the my-word-is-my-bond tradition of Friesland (my home province in the Netherlands), I loved truth, and the minister at the church had opened my eyes to the truth. According to the church, I was perfect in God's eyes, everything was OK, and I was not a bad person. That was the message Sunday after Sunday. So why was Gordon being so mean? After three hours of listening to me trying to explain myself with protests like: "But, but, but you don't understand" and "I know all that, but, but, but," Gordon turned to his assistant, Jacques, and asked, "What do you think of this creep?"

"Well, he's got a lot of problems," Jacques said. Until then, I'd thought Jacques was kind of nice. I didn't know why he would turn on me like that. Then Jody, the other assistant, said, "He's just not being real!" That did it: three against one. They were all nuts!

I don't know yet how to get out of here, but I'm sure there has got to be a taxi in town, I thought. I'm going to blow this place. The management is weird, the inmates are crazy. They all have major problems, and I'm not like that. My church friends have said that I am not like that.

Something must be wrong with the people who recommended this place. This place really sucks!

Gordon turned back to the rest of the group. "You have just seen what a classic case of denial is all about," he said. He then went around the room and asked what the rest thought of my performance. All twenty agreed that I was someone who was not willing to "own his stuff." Some of the comments annoyed me. Marie said that even though we were much the same age, I reminded her so much of her father that she had nothing but contempt for me and my attitudes towards my children and my former wife. Barbara from Mississippi, who I had thought was a very sweet woman, commented, "You keep hiding behind your religion and running from reality." Now, that hurt. This was exactly what I despised most about my father — that he hid behind religion. The next person to take a shot was Art from Seattle. If I had ever seen a loser, he was it, I thought, yet he accused me of taking everybody else's inventory except my own. What was he talking about? I had no inventory to take. He told me about his experience in Alcoholics Anonymous. As far as I was concerned, he was just the kind of creep that belonged there. Not I. I had nothing to worry about. Everything was fine with *me*.

At the end of the session, there was a thirty-minute break before supper. I went back to my room. My roommates, John and Harry, were now acting strange, real strange. Until now, I had been the clown in the room, I was the one who always made them laugh, but now they didn't respond to anything I tried. They said they didn't think I was funny. After they left, I just crawled into bed, and didn't bother going to eat supper.

I felt very cold. And very, very lonely. I had been lonely before in the past few years (ever since my divorce), but this was the ultimate loneliness. I stayed in bed the whole evening. I was getting my first taste of what it feels like to be a recluse. In the past few days I had heard a lot about the unhealthy practice of isolating. Now I was isolating myself, it seemed. But — no problem, I said to myself. In the morning I would get out of there. I'd have breakfast and then pack my bags and leave. I didn't have to put up with this.

I didn't sleep all night. The next morning, I announced to my roommates that I was leaving. Harry said, "Sure, run away. I am sure that's all you have ever done." I opened my mouth to tell him how wrong he was, then hesitated. I realized that he was right. What I was used to doing was running away if I didn't like something. I was also good at manipulating people to get what I wanted.

After my roommates left the room, I felt my gut aching with wanting to be right and to be loved. Even though it felt as though I was hated by everyone there, I stayed and somehow managed to get through the day. I didn't speak or associate with anyone. Even in the coffee breaks, I would go to bed. The comfort of a warm bed felt safe. As safe as being back in the womb. That is where I would like to have been. I sure wasn't feeling comfortable in the real world.

That day, in the classroom, I listened intently for the first time. I still wasn't agreeing with what was going on. I still had lots of judgments about the participants and the process. For instance, on the hot seat, Carl admitted that he had difficulty giving and receiving love. Gordon told him to hug a tree. How absurd, I thought.

That evening, as I did every evening, I walked around the lake, about two kilometres. This time, something made me leave the road and trudge through two feet of snow up a narrow path. After about two hundred yards, I stopped, staring at a particular tree which seemed to beckon to me. Slowly I walked up to the tree, remembering what Gordon had told Carl. I definitely wasn't going to hug the tree, so I just leaned against it. Standing there in the moonlight, in this winter wonderland, a calm came over me. I sensed that the tree was alive and I could feel it pulsing. This is silly, I thought. This is crazy. It just doesn't make any sense. I'd better get out of here!

How quiet it was! The snow crunching under my boots was the only sound to be heard. When I got back to the retreat centre, I didn't want to go in. I preferred staying outside where it was peaceful. I plodded around the lake again. On the second time around, I met six members of my group. Two casually nodded, but the other four ignored me. My God, I thought to myself, I hate this place. Why can't they be nice? Why can't they be sociable? I'm not a bad person. Besides, the things I confessed happened fifteen years ago. Why are they holding a grudge? Why?

After four trips around the lake, I went inside and joined in a game of Chinese checkers, but couldn't concentrate. After fifteen minutes, I left and went back to bed, feeling despair and loneliness like I'd never felt before. That night I slept two hours at most.

The next day's program was more sharing of our stories. By now I had decided to hang around for two more days, and hear some more stories, then leave. Instead of listening to the others, I spent much of the time trying to figure out how I could get them to understand my position. I had to find a way to show them what I was all about, tell them that I was not as bad as they thought.

My walks around the lake had stopped being a peaceful exercise. That night I trudged around the lake three times, and then once again headed up the path. The tree was a welcome sight. This is silly, I said to myself. How could I like a tree? I decided to sit in the snow underneath the tree. How silly I must look, I thought, sitting under a tree as if I were expecting a message from it. Still, there was something about this tree and the surroundings that felt immensely good. Just then I remembered the instruction to Carl: "Hug a tree." This time rather than just lean against the tree, I got up and hugged it. Before I knew it, I felt the tree hugging me back! The more I relaxed, the more I could feel the tree's life force. It was as though the tree and I had become one, exchanging energy. This is ridiculous, I thought, but at the same time I knew that it was happening and that it was true.

That evening in the recreation hall, Sally and Sue called me over to chat with them. I doubt that they had rehearsed what they wanted to say to me, but their approach was "good guy, bad guy," just like on a television police show, with one detective badgering and the other being understanding. Sally would say something like: "I know how it feels to be alone, I have been there myself, I know how it feels to be hurting." Then Sue would retort with: "Nobody but your self creates your own hurt, get real, smarten up!" Sally would say: "It will be fine, you'll feel better, this is just a rough time you're going through." Sue would say: "You deserve everything you get, you know." Probably for the first time in my life I listened, perhaps not well, but nevertheless listened. After twenty minutes of this, the three of us shared a hug. I was beginning to feel better. What amazed me was that I wasn't resentful or bitter towards Sue. I slept well that night.

The next day, however, I woke up resenting what Sue and Sally had said. They are so wrong about me, I thought. This place is getting to me if I even listened to them. I again started planning to leave. As usual, my roommates remained distant. On my way to the dining room, I ran into Jacques, the assistant director. He took one look at my face and said softly, "If ever you need any help, come and see me." Angrily I turned around and went the other way down the hall. Help? I don't need any help, I said to myself. Look at me: I'm successful, I've got it made, retired, doing whatever I want, and I'm only fifty-five years old. I've got everything I need. I don't need Jacques' help. I had lost my appetite, and decided to go for a walk.

Feeling dejected, I went around and around the lake. While walking I remembered a story my friend, Bob, had told me. When he was a sea captain, his ship was caught in a hurricane. For twelve hours he tried getting into the harbour. The dock had collapsed, the ship had run on the rocks and had lost its propeller. The battering of the storm had left the ship useless, stranded on the sandy beach. The next huge wave would smash it into the rocky shore. The ship as well as the passengers were doomed. There was nothing else Bob could do, so in anger he cried: "God, if you're there, you fix it!" The minute he screamed out that statement, he could feel a hot breath on the back of his neck. He looked around, but no one was there. At the same time, unbelievably, the boat began to slide off the beach and into the furious sea. Aimlessly it bounced around, then suddenly on the port side a dock appeared where Bob had seen none before. With virtually no steering left, the boat was almost certainly going to smash to pieces against the dock. Then the impossible happened — the boat started to respond to Bob's commands. He inched the boat gently into the dock and secured the lines. Everybody was safe. The moral of Bob's story was: When you become willing to surrender, a miracle will happen.

At first, I wondered why I was thinking of Bob's story. Then I realized that for the past two days, the instruction had been on the first three steps of Alcoholics Anonymous. Step One was: I can't. Step Two was: He can. Step Three was: Let Him. Was I willing to let Him? Was I willing to surrender, as Bob had with the boat? Really, I thought, God hasn't been that helpful to me in the past. I didn't think God even liked me. But I felt I had nowhere else to go. With as much feeling as I could muster, I said to myself, I can't, He can, and I'm going to let Him. I could feel myself surrendering! Suddenly, miraculously, inexplicably, all the burdens, all the weariness, disappeared. The unexpected peace was a tremendous relief.

Back at the residence, I found Jacques, and told him I was ready to surrender. He suggested I see Gordon. I was willing to tell Jacques that I was surrendering, but it was a different matter to tell Gordon. I was scared, and hesitated for some time. Was I going to lose my new-found resolve? I was petrified. Gordon's manner could be quite rough. Well, I thought, I've come this far, I might as well go for it. Anything was better than my experience of the past few days. I went to Gordon's office. Through my tears, I told him I was tired of the charade, and was tired of always wanting to be right. I was thirsting for a new way. Gordon said that he hoped that with the help of my Higher Power, I could look forward to a more peaceful existence. I felt it in my whole body. A new journey was about to begin.

Chapter 3

~

In Recovery

"You are now in recovery," they told me after twenty-eight days at the retreat in Montreal.

"Recovery from what?" I said. "I have given up drinking. What else is there?"

"How about your attitude?" they said.

"I have also changed that," I said. "What else do you want?"

"Well, for one thing, your arrogance . . ." they said.

That touched a nerve! I remembered where my arrogance had got me. I remembered where my lies had got me. I remembered where the drinking had got me. How quickly I had forgotten! I knew I had no choice but to learn more about recovery. At first, I thought transformation would be fun. How naive! Every time I thought I had all the answers, I discovered that I knew little or nothing. Sometimes I felt I finally had the answer to total honesty, only to discover that I was less than honest. I realized that I was attached to changing because to stagnate was not a viable state for me. It had led to major problems such as my use of alcohol.

Ever since the retreat in Montreal, I have been a diligent pupil, working on my recovery. I hope that by attending meetings and working with the twelve-step program, I can make compost out of my pile of garbage. But for the grace of God, I could easily be back in the emotional turmoil that results from my drinking, controlling, lying, arrogance, and all of my other character defects. I also know that I have to recover from the pain of my past. To heal the hurt I have suffered and in turn inflicted on others will probably take the rest of my life.

My experience at the retreat left me feeling cleansed, alive, and whole. The first Sunday I was back at church, I received a royal welcome from the other graduates of the retreat program. After the church service, we all met upstairs and I was asked to share my story of recovery. It felt terrific to be in the spotlight; I loved the recognition. I was proud and overjoyed when the minister welcomed me into the church's inner circle. I felt that I had arrived!

That evening I attended my first twelve-step program meeting. At the retreat, I had discovered that indeed I drank too much. My plan was to attend some twelve-step meetings for a year and then learn how to drink responsibly. It took three meetings of hearing other people's stories to know that to make it work, I had to buy the whole package. I had to admit that I was powerless over alcohol, and that my life was unmanageable. I knew that I didn't want to go through that insanity again. I surrendered to my Higher Power. I let go and let God. Regular meetings became part of my life, as did the Serenity Prayer: "God, grant me the serenity to accept the things I cannot change. The courage to change the things I can. And the wisdom to the know the difference."

Some time later, I was asked to be a leader for a twelve-step CODA (Co-dependents Anonymous) group. Gleefully, I accepted. I figured that at last I was being given a chance to show other people how great I was. My lifelong thirst for recognition could finally be quenched. I could be a wise and holy influence on others. After a few months, however, I finally began to feel uncomfortable with my assumption that I knew more than the other participants. At the next meeting of the CODA leaders, I shared my discomfort.

The group leaders were adamant in their position that it was necessary to guide and control the participants, and that graduates of the Montreal retreat were the ones to do the guiding and the controlling. Rather than gracefully accepting their verdict or even peacefully resigning, I allowed my niggling doubt to turn into a full-fledged over-reaction. Typical of my long history of extremes, my stubborn unwavering attitude got me fired from being a group leader and my recovery had a major setback. I instantly went into victim mode. Having played this role for fifty-five years, I knew it well. I also slipped in and out of the roles of martyr, judge, and crusader, but remained active in the church and the CODA group.

The church and the CODA group continued to teach me the lessons I needed to learn, however reluctantly. One weekend, the ministers called an assembly of graduates of the Montreal retreat. At this gathering it was announced that the two women who had been instrumental in my dismissal as a group leader had been fired, as well as banned, from the church. I must admit it felt good to be vindicated. Later, however, more people were requested to leave. The church which had once led me to the path of recovery was now falling apart. The place where I had experienced tremendous joy was now a war zone. The hatred I felt for some of the people in the CODA group and in the church and the sadness I felt about losing my major source of growth led me to look at my own role in what was happening.

Over the years, I had experienced quite a few disasters with organizations such as churches, strata councils, and Little League sports. Whenever I had been around groups, I had watched with a mixture of interest and sadness the dynamics that took place. What I saw was this: gossip ("Did you know what he/she did?"); agenda ("I think we should . . ."); bossiness ("You have to . . ."). I kept wanting to get on a soapbox and preach about a different world — the world according to me, but instead asked myself what I could learn from the current situation in the church.

I looked forward to the day when my recovery was advanced enough to observe others with love and understanding, but realized that I still had the impulse to judge what I saw and heard rather than accepting what was. Was it possible that a shake-up and a wake-up in *my* thinking was due? I realized that I had again slipped into some unhealthy patterns — needing to be right, wanting control, feeling victimized, being self-righteous, and over-reacting. It was so easy to see where everyone else erred, but where was *I* going wrong? Probably with all of the above, but foremost, I knew, was my need to control. When I could acknowledge that I was responsible for my part in any power struggle, my recovery started to get back on track.

While this inward and outward struggle was going on, my father died. He was the most accomplished "controller" I had ever known. The night before the funeral, the family gathered for a viewing. Most of my siblings were present. I didn't know if they felt what I felt, which certainly was not grief. At the same time, the anger, bitterness, and contempt which I had felt in the past seemed dormant. It had been three years since I had seen my father. When I walked up to the open coffin, I was shocked to discover how I resembled him physically. Standing at the foot of his coffin, I resolved that if at all possible, when my time came to leave this plane, people would not feel the indifference that I was experiencing now about my father. During the graveside ceremony, one of my sisters remained dry-eyed, and whispered to me: "I hated him." At the post-funeral get-together, rather than talking about the departed's good deeds, the conversation was about how he had failed to make contact with his children.

The experience left me with a thirst for a higher quality of life while I was still alive. I knew that with my skill at controlling and manipulating, I too had caused others a great deal of pain. What will I do, I wondered, when people, places and things disappoint me? Get even? React? Defend? Or can I change all that? One thing I knew is that the journey of recovery kept opening up new avenues. All I had to do was follow.

Section 2

≈

Looking For
the Miracle-workers
of India

Chapter 4

~

Why India?

People often ask me why I have chosen to go so many times to India. My answer can be traced back to an evening early in the fall of 1991. A dozen of us were shouting, "Bend, bend, bend!" Each of us was holding the tip of a spoon between the thumb and fourth finger of our hands. We were trying to bend the spoon with the power of our minds, not with the strength in our fingers.

I glanced over at some of the others who had already succeeded in bending their spoons into a pretzel or ball shape. We had been told at the start not to apply pressure or force the spoon to bend. Since my spoon was not bending, I decided to apply pressure, but there just was not enough strength between my thumb and finger to bend the spoon. One by one, the other participants were bending their spoons. I was becoming increasingly frustrated by my lack of progress. Maybe my spoon was thicker than the others? Maybe they were cheating?

Just as I was about to give up, and started to relax, my spoon started getting warm. When I felt the heat and released the spoon, it fell to the ground. By now six of the participants had bent their spoons. I was encouraged enough by this to pick up the spoon and focus again. After ten minutes or so, the spoon suddenly became totally elastic and I rolled it into a small ball. A parlour game? No, we were in a Vancouver church. The leader that evening was Dr. Brian O'Leary, Ph.D., a scientist, astronaut, author, and lecturer. He was demonstrating how the human mind, either individually or collectively, has tremendous power.

At the conclusion of the evening, Brian O'Leary extended an invitation to anyone interested in joining him on a journey to India. The purpose of his trip, he said, was to find the miracle-workers of India, who were to be part of the research for a book he was writing. In awe with what I had experienced that evening, I decided to go.

At the Vancouver church I attended, I had heard many times that the power of the human mind can defeat dreaded diseases like cancer or AIDS. Long before I ever heard of this church, however, I had been hearing tales about the miracle-workers in India — people who could charm snakes without being bitten, people who could lie on beds of nails without being hurt — and had been wanting to see these miracles first-hand. In fact, a year earlier, while travelling in Asia, I had had a visa for entering India, but some of my fellow travellers persuaded me not to go, saying that they were sure I would not enjoy it. I had regretted that decision ever since.

Having finally decided to go to India, I began to question my motives as well as my sanity. After the experience of bending the spoon, my interest in the human mind and its potential was at an all-time high. But was my interest really in the miracle-workers? Why was I interested? Did I expect to learn how to walk on water, as well as bend spoons, so that I could show everyone how enlightened I was? Or did I think I was going to save heathens? I knew that to some extent all of these were true, but I also knew that I was driven by curiosity and that my thirst for experiences would educate me. A few weeks later, I was on my way.

I soon discovered that for me, going to India was more than finding miracle-workers. India would give me an education, but not in the way I had thought. India was not only going to teach me a lot about patience, non-reaction, and non-judgment, but heal a lot of hurt in me. With all of its sights and sounds, its people and its culture, India awakened in me a compassion I didn't know existed. Over the next six years, I saw India from the splendour of the Taj Mahal to the squalor of Calcutta. I learned to let India teach me. Sometimes the teacher was a dying man, a rickshaw puller in Calcutta, another volunteer; other times, it was an Indian doctor, or someone associated with Mother Teresa. Saints such as Mother Teresa and Sai Baba spoke loudly to me, and I listened. I listened and learned. What I experienced in India made me cry, and made me laugh, but most importantly, it changed me forever, and the change was profound. Gradually, my thirst for power and excitement changed into a thirst for understanding and compassion. My gratitude knows no bounds.

Chapter 5

~

Sacred Places

Where is the sacred? Some find the sacred in a temple, mosque or church. Others are convinced they experience it on a mountain top, a beach, a busy street or office. And what is the sacred? I am still trying to explore these questions, but for me, the sacred can be a holy being or a holy place or thing devoted or consecrated to a holy being or some other divine purpose. A holy being can be Allah, Buddha, Krishna, God, or any Higher Power, internal or external. I believe that whatever is sacred must also be nurturing. I certainly do not find all so-called sacred approaches nurturing. For example, having experienced what I call "the doom-and-gloom approach" for many years, I now consider that message anything but sacred. When a leader in any church uses terms like "We beseech Thee," "Have mercy," "Forgive us," "We are not worthy," or "Pleeeeease," I want to escape and head for the pure mountain air.

Since travel has been a major part of my life for many years, I have seen many of the world's most renowned sacred places, including the great cathedrals of Europe, and the Vatican. In some of those places I have felt a presence that is difficult to explain. Other times, I have been deeply moved simply by the music of a great pipe organ. I have felt the vibration in my bones. Similarly, I have stood in a vortex in Sedona, Arizona, and experienced emotional and physical vibrations.

On a few occasions I have attended a church a in Santa Monica, California, where I have also experienced a meaningful worship experience. At that church, there is a dynamic preacher, a talented and enthusiastic music director, a band, and a one-hundred-and-seventy-voice choir. Together, they create a magical encounter through high-energy music, effective speaking, and always some humour. I love the quantity and high quality of the hugs I receive there. I feel full of joy and happiness. It's my kind of a place, but I have found this kind of church experience to be rare in the West. I plan to take my thirst for the sacred to the Middle East, Greece and Israel, and to Peru's Machu Picchu — and to revisit Sedona, Arizona. This chapter is about some of my experiences of the sacred places — and the not-so-sacred — in India, because they have affected me the most so far.

Travelling to India didn't allow me to escape the clutches of the doom-and-gloom approach. One day, I was asked to attend a play at a church on Park Street in Calcutta. That night the platform was divided into three sections: one side was Heaven, the other was Hell, and in between were a number of angels. One angel held a huge book. In the opening scene, an old woman appeared and shared with us how she loved the Lord. Suddenly, she fell down and died. Next, there was soft music and the old woman appeared before the angel holding the book. The angel indicated that the old woman should take the door to the right (Heaven) and the choir sang hallelujahs.

The next scene involved two teen-age girls.

"You should go to church," one said to the other.

"No, I party late Saturday nights and I am always hung over, and church is boring," the other retorted.

Next, there were loud noises — BANG, CRASH! — and the girls were knocked down by a car. Then they too appeared in front of the angel holding the book. The angel looked up the name of the churchgoing girl and gave her a huge smile and pointed to Heaven, and the choir sang hallelujahs. Next the angel checked the book for the name of the party girl. The angel frowned and pointed to Hell. The party girl pleaded, but the angel was firm and pointed again to Hell. Imitation fires started burning and the devil (dressed in black and carrying a red pitchfork) emerged from the flames. With a piercing and wicked laugh, he dragged the party girl off to Hell.

Over the evening, many similar scenes were portrayed. I found the last one the most oppressive. A mother and her six-year-old daughter appeared before the angel. The mother was sent to Hell (for lack of church attendance). While the devil with his vicious cackle was dragging the mother off to Hell, the little girl was screaming, "Mummy, Mummy!" End of play!

The minister dashed onto the platform, ran over to the microphone and said, "Thiiiiiiis could happen to you!" For the next fifteen minutes, he begged people to come to the front and kneel so that he could pray for them.

"If you don't come," he shouted, "you have seen what will happen. It says so in the Biiiiiible!"

I was amazed to see how many responded to his approach of using fear to bring people to God. What was truly absurd, I almost slithered to the front myself! Stirring up alarm and fear was very effective and it almost succeeded in winning my soul. For weeks this play had an effect on me. My primary emotion was anger, with perhaps a niggling doubt.

In contrast, another time I was travelling with a group and we were asked whether we would like to meet the High Priest of a Hindu temple. Having expressed our interest, we were taken upstairs in the temple and served tea. We chatted with an ordinary priest for about an hour, during which time he tried to explain the rather complicated Hindu religion. Then word came that the High Priest couldn't see us for some time. We could wait, or leave. We decided to leave, since we had deadlines to meet. As we were getting ready to go, we could hear bells in the temple downstairs. The priest said, "Temple services are about to begin. Would you like to observe?" Again, we said yes. We were taken down a set of stairs that led onto the altar, and were told to stay on the platform where a priest was burning incense. In the front of the altar stood two men bare to the waist. Each was holding up a large metal gong which they took turns beating. The noise was deafening, and yet inspiring.

Everyone in the temple was standing, and it was so crowded that the walls seemed about to be pushed out. Many of the worshippers were screaming and swaying, and as the tempo of the gongs increased, the noise from the worshippers increased. The room was poorly lit. To me, it felt eerie, yet I could also feel a strange energy in the room. We watched for a half an hour, then our leader indicated it was time to leave. As we walked outside, I noticed for the first time a long railing. It looked like a hitching rail in cowpoke movies, only this one didn't have horses on it. There were people handcuffed to it. Even though these people were outside the temple, they too were swaying to the rhythm of the gongs. Our priest guide explained that what we were witnessing was an exorcism, an attempt to drive out evil spirits. Those on the railing were potentially dangerous and were kept outside to protect those inside. In this temple, apparently, the method for driving out evil spirits was noise and hype. (At a previous temple, we had observed an exorcism by self-flagellation, where a young woman kept throwing herself against a concrete floor while letting out agonizing groans.) The priest explained that these people, like most in India, were too poor to afford a psychiatrist, and this was their way of therapy. Watching the gyrations and feeling the emotions of the participants was a powerful experience, even though I didn't know if it was effective as a cure.

In my travels to sacred places, I often found Hindu temples rather gaudy. To me, the gods and goddess looked like they were from outer space. One looked like a monkey, another like an elephant. Others had many arms and legs, and most were adorned with bright colours. Although I didn't understand the religion well, I sensed an aura of serenity around those that practised Hindu teachings. Unfortunately, on a few occasions I inadvertently offended a Hindu priest by declining to take holy food (prasad) or holy water. Often the water came from the lethal waters of the River Ganges, and I didn't want to risk the potential health problems.

India was dotted with Hindu holy places, and the devout went to these special places on certain holidays or other occasions. These groups could number in the millions or just be a handful of people. In Calcutta, I often worked in the same building that housed a famous temple devoted to Kali (also known as Kali Ma, the Hindu Triple Goddess of creation, preservation, and destruction). This temple was unique among the temples I had seen. For one thing, live sacrifices (goats) were beheaded in a small fenced area inside the temple. For another, after the guided tours, extreme pressure was applied to pry a large donation from visitors.

The Kali temple was always a beehive of activity, and on special feast days was jammed to capacity, with pilgrims arriving by the bus- or truck-load from outside Calcutta. The pilgrims from the villages stuck out amongst the city folk. Many were barefoot and carried burlap or plastic bags on top of their heads. Looking bewildered with all the noise, people, and buildings, they walked in groups, usually following a leader. Their purpose was mostly to visit the temple, but sometimes they also participated in a political rally. They cooked, ate, and slept together, often close to the transportation they had used to get to the city: a train, an open truck, or a beat-up bus. Hundreds camped on the railway station platforms or in parking lots. On the holy River Ganges, where many major religious events took place, a city of a million people could spring up overnight and disappear just as quickly. The only mementos were the mountains of garbage left behind.

In the sacred Hindu city of Varanasi, which I visited one time, I felt I was on holy ground. Here most of the activity was near the River Ganges, where naked sadhus (Hindu wandering holy men) sat and meditated or gave counsel to seekers of spiritual truth, mostly Westerners. Here the river was lined with burning ghats, a Hindu way of burial. As I understood it, to die in Varanasi meant rebirth on a higher level.

Where Hindu temples seemed gaudy, the Muslim mosques seemed the other extreme. They were very plain, yet what they lacked in appearance was made up for by the piety of the worshippers. Rarely did I live anywhere in India where I couldn't hear the Muslim call to prayer five times a day. The call consisted of a male voice magnified many times by loud speakers repeating the message that it was time to pray. In the services, there was a lot of bowing, but no singing or dancing.

I also travelled to three major Buddhist sacred sites: Bodgaya, the place where the Buddha received enlightenment under the Bodhi tree; Dharamsala, where the Dalai Lama lived in exile from Tibet; and Leh, in Ladakh in the far north of India. In Bodgaya and Dharamsala, there were many Westerners intensely pursuing the sacred. In fact, in Bodgaya the only industry seemed to be Buddhism. There were many temples, meditation centres and, of course, there was the famous Bodhi tree. My visit there was too short to leave any impact.

I also spent only a short time in Dharamsala, but decided it would warrant a return visit. Ten miles from Dharamsala was a hilltop retreat called Mcleod Ganj where the Dali Lama's palace was located. It was surrounded by hotels and restaurants catering mostly to the Westerners who had come to see and hear the Dali Lama. I could feel the energy of a sacred tradition that had survived for twenty-five hundred years.

In Leh, every few miles there were monasteries, some large and some small. Only one was less than a hundred years old. Another had existed for fifteen hundred years. Each of the six that I visited was unique and in some I could feel an awesome energy. One place that felt sacred was a room where a three-storey-high Buddha was residing. The native population in Leh was mostly Tibetan. Many wore heavy maroon coats (it was winter) and had a mala (string of prayer beads) wrapped around one wrist. Most used the mala as they walked around, their lips moving in prayer while their fingers manipulated the beads on the string. Virtually everyone was walking and praying. I had the feeling that I was walking on holy ground there.

My most memorable experience there was at prayer time at the Japanese Gompa on a hill just above Leh. I arrived just as the service was about to begin. The room was small and on the altar were several Buddha figures with Japanese facial features. These were different from the Tibetan statues I had been visiting. The room also contained two huge drums, one on each side of the room. Two laymen began to pound the drums and chant. A priest sitting next to me on the floor had a smaller drum. I too was handed a drum.

Not having experienced drumming before, I felt awkward. Once I got into the rhythm, however, I felt better, and as my confidence increased, I was able to close my eyes or look at the Buddha statues. One particular sculpture seemed to be staring at me. I was mesmerized by it. The tempo of the drumming escalated. I found the drumming and the chanting very moving. I felt totally in tune with the room and the drums, and I felt a heaviness in me disappear. Until that moment, I hadn't realized that I was feeling heavy! Just as I was about to float heavenward, the music stopped abruptly. Glassy-eyed, I left the temple vowing to sometime, somewhere, re-enact this experience.

Chapter 6

≈

Enlightenment

For the past several years, I have had a tremendous passion for the person who claimed to be enlightened. Whenever such a person came to town, I rushed out and bought tickets (and I still do). I hoped I might actually receive some new insight, or see a miracle, but most often I showed myself to be a skeptic. I would sit there waiting for her or him to be human and make an error and then I was totally unforgiving. Often I judged the person to be phoney before he or she had even said a word.

One reason I was so quick to judge was that I was so attached to the idea that enlightenment was God-like perfection, or all-knowing. One day I decided to expand my way of thinking by looking the word up in a few dictionaries. *Webster's New Dictionary* (1990) defined enlightenment as "free from prejudice or superstition." The *Random House Dictionary* (1968) defined it as giving "spiritual or intellectual light" to others, and teaching or imparting knowledge. And *Collins Compact Dictionary* (1994) said that enlightenment had "beneficial effects." While including these perspectives did not prevent me from being skeptical, it helped me become more open in my way of thinking about enlightenment.

In addition to thinking about what enlightenment meant, I was interested in the question: Which of the past and current miracle-workers or gurus were enlightened? I continued seeking out the followers of Christ, Buddha, Osho, Sai Baba, Mother Teresa . . . there was a long list. Even though I was trying to expand my definition of enlightenment, I still couldn't decide who was truly enlightened. And to make my confusion worse, many followers claimed that their guru was the right one! What to do? My Calvinist tradition said that one had to be wrong and one had to be right. Could they both be wrong? Or both right?

In the past few years, most of the people with whom I have been associating have been following enlightened beings or working feverishly to become enlightened themselves. I too have been caught up in the search for enlightenment, as this section will show, and I probably will be again, but mostly now I don't care much one way or the other. The day I began not to care was while on a trip from Puri to Calcutta, and that day I experienced a new joy and a new serenity. (I begin this chapter with that story.) In that moment, I became free to listen any master or teacher that felt right. I could adopt what I liked and reject what didn't feel right, without judgment. I treasure those moments whenever they happen.

$\sim$

One day in 1995, on a trip from the resort town of Puri to the city of Calcutta, I was privileged to share a first-class train compartment with a man wearing the orange robes of a guru. After hours of conversation, I got up enough courage to ask him, "Are you enlightened?"

"You will have to ask my followers," he replied.

"I asked *you*," I said, feeling very daring.

"In some areas, I guess I am," he said, after a thoughtful pause. I loved his answer. The longer I reflected on it, the more sense it made to me, and the more curious I became. How did one get enlightened? The more I wondered about it, the more I didn't know! When a Christian talked about a new birth or a born-again experience, was that enlightenment? Or could a person become enlightened by meditating, reading, studying, or praying, as some advocated? Did the earth move when it happened? Did the person go into convulsions? Or did something else happen physically?

An experience I had in Pune, India, gave me yet another definition of enlightenment and was perhaps the closest I came to experiencing enlightenment myself. I was sitting at a darshan (an audience given by an enlightened being). Most of the attendees were Westerners like myself and most were in Pune for the Osho ashram. After a meditation, the enlightened teacher invited questions from the audience. I loved all of his answers as well as his style. At this session, most of the questions were variations on one theme: "How does one become enlightened?" And each time the answer would boil down to: "Just be." The audience response to this answer was something like: "That's too simple," or "I haven't taken enough courses yet," or "I'm too young." The objections were many and varied. It seemed the Western mind didn't like simple answers! In one instance, a man was getting very angry and frustrated with the answers. The teacher was kindly and patient, but the questioner persisted, determined to get an answer that would suit him. To try and deflect the man's anger, the teacher asked the man to fly with him over Pune. That was the last straw — the man was sure he couldn't fly without an airplane.

In the meantime, I was fully in tune with the enlightened teacher, and accepted the offer to fly with him. My body remained seated, but I was hovering for a few minutes over the assembled crowd. It seemed like a most natural thing to do. I can't explain why I had this feeling or how it happened. Was it just an illusion? I don't know. I wasn't drunk or on drugs. Was it because I was in tune with the teacher and didn't doubt that I could?

～

A few years have passed since that experience and nothing has happened like that since. I thirst for more and more experiences of this type so that I might be convinced that this was an experience of enlightenment. Just as the other participants were raising objections, I still struggle with my own doubts. When I flew, I knew I could. If only I could allow myself more times to "just be." And to remind myself that I can be whatever I want. Perhaps my friend on the train was right, that we can experience enlightenment on some things and not on others. I have learned well how to be in control, and this seems directly opposite to "just being." Maybe, for me, each time I surrender my need to be in control I experience enlightenment.

Chapter 7

❦

Sai Baba

On January 8, 1992, I left Vancouver for my first trip to India. I spent three days poking around Singapore. I enjoyed browsing in the shops and exploring the offerings of the many outdoor eating establishments and also experimented with taking buses to various parts of the city. Singapore became my first stop for many trips to Asia, and was to become like a second home.

Three days later, I went to the airport to meet for the first time my travelling companions arriving from Los Angeles. The group consisted of four men and four women (none were related), and all had responded to Brian O'Leary's talks about the miracle-workers of India. Excited about the journey we were about to undertake, we boarded a plane for New Delhi, India, where we met with more travelling companions who had arrived earlier that day from New York. Our group was now complete.

❦

All thirteen of us had been inspired by Brian O'Leary's lecture tour. We instantly bonded into a congenial group, all having in common a thirst to experience miracles. The first ten days we did the things tourists do, such as visit temples, shrines, ashrams, and, of course, the Taj Mahal. On January 22, we were scheduled to meet with Sai Baba, one of the most famous miracle-workers alive. I was skeptical. I had heard many rumours about fake holy men. One was said to have spent time in jail and been deported from the United States.

My thoughts about Sai Baba were that he was probably a phoney as well. Still, I was curious to see what miracles he could perform. Before arriving in India, I had never heard of him. For some of my travelling companions, on the other hand, the primary purpose for being on the trip was to meet Sai Baba and experience his miracles.

Two days before meeting with Sai Baba, we flew to Bangalore for a free day, enabling us to rest and reflect on our ten days of sights and experiences. At the airport, a chartered bus was ready for us. While waiting for our luggage, we bombarded Ajit, our driver, with questions about Sai Baba. Ajit suggested we meet with his father-in-law, an avid devotee of Sai Baba. Eagerly we accepted his proposal. Ajit went into the airport to find out what had happened to our luggage and to see whether he could arrange a visit with his father-in-law. When Ajit came back, he announced that our luggage had gone to Goa, and might arrive in Bangalore on an evening flight. If we were still interested, we could meet with his father-in-law now. We accepted, boarded the bus, and feasted our eyes on the wide, clean, tree-lined streets and many parks.

Ajit drove us to a street with large, beautifully maintained houses and stopped in front of a house with an impressive iron gate. A distinguished-looking gentleman welcomed us to his home and his country. His name was Mr. Srutaiya. He ushered us into his living room and invited us to sit down. Since we were such a large group, some of us sat on the floor. Two cultured and elegant women, his wife and his mother, served tea and sweets.

For the next three hours, our host shared his life story as well as his experiences with Sai Baba. He told us that his wife had been a devotee of Sai Baba twelve years before he was. When Mr. Srutaiya's son turned eight, Mrs. Srutaiya wanted to take him to Baba for a ceremonial haircut. At first, Mr. Srutaiya refused to go, but later consented to preserve matrimonial harmony. When Baba and Mr. Srutaiya met, their eyes locked. Mr. Srutaiya instantly knew that he had met his teacher. On another occasion he sat in a large hall near the back, listening to Sai Baba speak. Mr. Srutaiya had a severe headache. The pain was excruciating. Unexpectedly, Baba walked from the front of the room to the back, smiled at Mr. Srutaiya, and touched his head. Instantly the pain was gone. A miracle? It was to Mr. Srutaiya. He also talked at length about how he and others had defied the British during their rule. The main strategy was to agree to do something, and then not follow through. This created a lot of frustration for the British and caused a great deal of inefficiency.

Before we left his house, Mr. Srutaiya led us into his devotion room where he taught us some Hindu songs and devotional practices. When we left the house, I was floating in a blissful state. What a privilege to experience a man with so much love and caring, as well as to be introduced to a new culture and a religious practice that was so genuine and inspiring. I'd had no experience with Eastern religions and had been naive enough to believe that Western religions were the only ones that counted. In my earlier Calvinistic upbringing, those who didn't have that same religion were considered heathens. This belief was being put to the test, for I was falling in love with India and its people, and my indifference to Sai Baba was changing into anticipation.

The next day, after being reunited with our luggage, we boarded the bus once again. This time our destination was Sai Baba's ashram at Puttaparthi. In spite of the bumpy road, the journey into the countryside was very pleasant, with rice paddies all along our route, as well as mango, coconut, and banana trees. Puttaparthi is in the state of Andhra Pradesh, about one hundred and fifty kilometres from Bangalore. On the road to Puttaparthi, we met an entourage of six vehicles led by a shiny gold-coloured Mercedes. Since this type of automobile was rare in India, and particularly so on this bumpy country road, our bus driver speculated that Sai Baba might have been in the car. And indeed, when we arrived at the ashram we were told that we had just missed Baba.

Some people in our group were devastated to have missed seeing him. I was only mildly upset as the ride to our destination had been very pleasant and I was enjoying looking around at the ashram. Before our arrival we had been led to believe that we were going to a small village. Puttaparthi was anything but a small village. It contained many large buildings: residences for the pilgrims, many levels of schools, hospitals, a research centre, and a recently built airstrip. The main streets were jammed with souvenir shops and eating places as well as the usual merchants. On the hillside surrounding Puthaparti were huge statues of Jesus, Buddha, Krishna, and others I did not recognize. The statues seemed to be standing guard over the town and ashram below. As I walked within the walls of the ashram, I had the feeling I was walking on sacred ground. Lush green shrubs and colourful flowers lined the pathways. Everywhere small signs on sticks were stuck into flower beds. On each sign was written a quotation from Baba. The ashram contained some exquisite buildings, including Sai Baba's residence and a large two-storey building beautifully decorated with ornate and colourful woodwork. Any king, queen, or pope would be proud to appear on one of the balconies and let the throngs below pay homage. The library, although closed for renovations, was another marvellous building, its exterior embellished by larger-than-life statues of a blue elephant and golden lions, fancy pillars and doorways.

In contrast, for the thousands of pilgrims staying at the ashram, the accommodations were dormitory-style: six persons to a room. Mattresses were two inches thick and laid directly on the floor. Food was served in a large dining hall, buffet-style. Chairs and tables were plain and made out of wood. After eating, everyone was asked to wash dishes or clean up. The cost for a stay — although inexpensive by Western standards — was almost double the going rate in the area.

One of the buildings on the property was a very long, narrow building with doors every few feet. Upon close inspection I discovered that this was a latrine building. Since we were about to start our return journey, I thought it wise to go to the toilet. This facility consisted of a hole in the ground and nothing else. The first four "toilets" I checked out were filthy with piles of excrement. I stepped back in disgust and decided to wait. We boarded the bus back to Bangalore.

One hour into our journey we got off the bus for a pit stop, as many others also had decided to forego the toilets at the ashram. We trekked into the fields to fertilize the crops. The evening sky was dark purple, the sun was bright red and orange. We stood on the road, transfixed by this awesome sight. I could feel an indescribable, powerful energy. Others said they felt the same, and used words like eerie, intense, chilling, charged, awesome, and startling. What was this experience? Was it spiritual?

On the second day of our pursuit of the elusive Sai Baba, we learned that he had moved to another ashram, Whitefield, just fifteen kilometres away from our hotel. Mr. Srutaiya joined us on our visit to Whitefield and once again was very helpful. While we waited, he went to some people in charge of the ashram and talked with them, and in no time we were escorted passed the waiting crowds and seated in the front row. To our surprise, the women had to sit in a different section. They protested as they felt discriminated against, but agreed to follow the local customs and sat in the women's section. The crowds continued to pour in and waited on the gravel-covered ground for the arrival of their idol. Fortunately, most of our group had bought pillows from the vendors who had besieged our bus as we arrived.

Sitting behind me was a group all wearing kerchiefs of the same colour. I eavesdropped on their conversation and discovered that they were Dutch. I turned around to talk with them and learned that they had come from Holland together. They pointed out several other groups from Germany, France, and Ireland. One member of the Dutch group had been coming for twenty years and stayed several weeks at a time, always hoping that someday he might get a audience with Baba. Some of the crowd were chatting, others sat quietly. Still others were in deep meditation. Finally, I too sat quietly and immediately started to feel the energy of the crowd. It was like nothing I'd ever felt before.

I kept pushing the feeling away. My Dutch Reformed background was warning me not to get involved. At the same time, I wouldn't have missed this for the world. To see a real saint, to physically touch an avatar, a god in human form! Was he an authentic god or a fake? I knew that thousands, perhaps millions, of people from all over the world were followers. In the midst of my inner turmoil, I suddenly heard stirring music coming from a building that looked like a palace. The noisy crowd hushed and the energy in the compound felt as though it was about to explode. Slowly, the double doors in the white-washed brick fence opened. The tension was almost unbearable.

Slowly, slowly, a small figure in an orange robe and an Afro hairstyle approached the waiting audience. The crowd of thousands collectively took a deep breath. Some were crying; I also wanted to cry, but suppressed it. The figure came closer and closer. When he was just a few feet away from my group, he lifted his hand, and from his fingertips sprayed a grayish powder called vibhuti over the devotees. The crowd came alive with movement, people catching the spray, rubbing themselves with it, or even eating it. Some handed him letters, sweets, money, and many other items. I was overwhelmed. He stopped in front of where we were sitting, looked us over carefully, pointed to the palace gate, and said: "Go."

There was much confusion in our small group. What were we to do? I didn't want to leave, especially not knowing where he was sending us. But we decided to follow Mr. Srutaiya, who was already leading the way towards the palace. The women from our group, who were sitting in the women's section, had their own confusion about what to do. They decided to follow the rest of us.

As soon as we arrived at the palace gates, we were told to wait to the left of the building. After fifteen minutes, Sai Baba came back through the gate and headed for a group of young men dressed in white Indian garb. He chatted with some and gave blessings to others. They were students at Whitefield College, located in the ashram. After visiting with the students, he went up the steps and through the front door of the palace. We were disappointed. Was that all we would get to see of him? But soon Sai Baba reappeared at a side door near where we were standing, and told us to come in. Now we were only a few feet away from him. Some of our group got down on their knees to touch or kiss his feet. Once again I felt a strong resistance. This type of behaviour seemed excessive to me.

The room we entered was plain, like many rooms in India. All it contained was a wooden coffee table with a glass top. At the end of the table stood a large wing chair covered with red velvet which gave it the look of a throne. The walls, covered with a cream-coloured whitewash, had no paintings, wall hangings or any other type of adornment. We were directed to sit on the concrete floor at the foot of the red velvet chair. And again, as is the custom in India, the women were on the left and the men on the right. When we were seated, Baba walked among us and sprayed us with vibhuti until the supply stopped flowing from his fingertips. He seated himself on the red velvet chair and started a lecture. He talked about the skies and clouds and technology. I was mesmerized.

Suddenly, Sai Baba turned to Brian O'Leary and asked him about space travel. You could see Sai Baba's disappointment when Brian told him that although he was in the space program, he had never gone into outer space. Sai Baba then asked Brian if he would like a diamond ring and received a very enthusiastic yes. Sai Baba stretched out his hand, palm down, and began to rotate his wrist. After a few seconds, he turned his hand up, and held between his fingers a diamond ring, which he handed to Brian. Brian put the ring on his finger, admired it, and turned it around. He was beaming with joy. Sai Baba watched Brian play with the ring, then asked, "It is a little large, isn't it? Hold up your hand." Brian held his hand up. Sai Baba touched the ring, and said, "Now try it." The ring, instead of flopping around on Brian's finger, now fit perfectly.

Next, Sai Baba directed his attention to Yas, one of the women in our group, and said: "Your blood will be just fine." She replied: "There is nothing wrong with my blood." Until then, I hadn't realized that I wanted Sai Baba to fail, but at that moment something in me said: See, he *is* phoney. Once again Sai Baba stretched out his hand, revolved his wrist, and a large chunk of rock candy popped into his hand. He offered it to Yas, who inspected it closely.

"Is this sugar?" she asked Sai Baba. He replied that it was.

"I can't eat this," Yas objected, "I'm a diabetic."

"I know," Sai Baba assured her. "Go ahead and eat it and your blood will be just fine."

A few minutes ago, I had been skeptical that Sai Baba was more than just a good magician, but now I was impressed. We spent an hour with Sai Baba, talking and asking questions. After that, we were led into another room where the ashram photographer took our pictures.

While in this room, Marie, a member of our group, received a healing from Sai Baba for an ailment she'd had for five years. The meeting ended with Baba shaking hands with each of us. When it was my turn, as I shook his hand, he looked at me with penetrating eyes. He knows! I thought. I knew that I couldn't hide my skepticism from him.

~

For the rest of our trip, the group had many discussions about what we had seen and experienced with Sai Baba. Yas stopped taking insulin with no ill effects, but after a number of days, a doctor travelling with us convinced her that it was best to start taking it again. For a time, I considered becoming a devotee of Sai Baba.

When we returned to New Delhi, we had a meeting with another holy man called Sayed Shamsuddin Baba Altamas. For three hours, we observed his healing touch and asked him questions. When asked if he knew Sai Baba, he sent one of his devotees to get a photo album. In the album were pictures of a younger Sai Baba, who had been his student. Sayed Shamsuddin Baba Altamas said that he was not pleased with Sai Baba — Sai Baba had become too commercial and had lost his humility. Hearing this was a shock to me and turned around any desire to follow Sai Baba. Since I had my own struggles with submission, I said to myself, I didn't need to follow someone who wasn't humble.

Chapter 8

~

Divine Light

It was now May 1992. I was slicing tomatoes and chopping carrots at a kitchen counter, helping prepare dinner. My thoughts were on my recent trip to India. Ten months ago I'd joined a group and we were in a wind-up retreat on beautiful Galiano Island. From the window we had a fantastic view of Trincomali Channel. The house was only a hundred feet from the water. In between the house and the rocky cliffs leading to the water was a thatched roof hut. I asked our host, Gitananda, who was standing near me, what the hut was used for.

"For meditation," she replied.

"I wish I could learn how to meditate," I said wistfully.

"I will teach you." she said. "Every Wednesday, I teach yoga at the ashram in Vancouver."

"Isn't yoga a type of exercise?" I asked. "And what does that have to do with meditation?"

"From Yoga we learn pranayama, or breathing," she replied. "After that comes meditation, and from there we go to the divine light within."

As soon as she mentioned "divine light," I was hooked. Without hesitation I decided to join the Wednesday night group. It sounded exactly what I had been looking for!

While we continued to chop vegetables, I noticed Gitananda's clothes. She was wearing what looked like a sort of track suit: baggy pants and a loose-fitting long-sleeved top. Both garments were formless and the orange colour was badly faded. Had the colour been bright orange, I might have noticed her outfit earlier. I was curious, and finally mustered up enough courage to ask whether there was any significance to the clothes. In a modest tone of voice she said, "Yes, I'm a swami in the Puri lineage and my teacher is Paramhans Swami Maheshwarananda." Wow! I was chopping veggies with a real swami who was wearing plain clothes and sporting short hair.

I continued to ask questions. One story in particular sent shivers down my spine. Gitananda was standing, she said, on the very spot we were now, and she was preparing dinner. Gazing out the window, she saw an orange-clad figure walking up the road towards her house, and went out to greet him. He said, "Follow me." I could hardly believe my ears. I remembered from my childhood that there was a very similar story in the Bible. I longed for such an event to occur in my life. I craved such clarity. Everything felt uncertain to me at the time. To hear that such things can still happen in the twentieth century shook me and gave me hope that it could happen to me one day.

Later that day, I retreated to the meditation hut. I watched the mink play on the rocks below and gazed at the water rolling gently on the shore. In that state of tranquillity I believe I experienced meditation for the first time. A calm came over me, a peacefulness, and a knowing that there was a way out, even for me. Would my yearning for serenity finally be fulfilled?

~

The following Wednesday, I arrived fifteen minutes early at the address Gitananda had given me. I had been expecting to see a large building like a temple, but what I saw was just a house in the middle-class subdivision of Kerrisdale. While still in my car, I saw a young woman walking down the block. I got out of the car and asked her if she knew where the ashram was. With a smile she said, "This is it! Are you going to yoga?" I nodded. "Come with me," she said.

We walked in the front door without knocking, and hung our coats in the closet. We took our shoes off and lined them up with the others. There were two doorways. The woman pointed me to the one on the right. I watched her go into the one on the left, then peeked in after her. On the altar inside, some incense was burning, and there were a few pictures of orange-robed holy men. I found out later that this room was called the puja room, and that it was used for devotion or prayer.

I went into the yoga room on the right. Inside, cushions and blankets were piled on the floor, and a ghettoblaster was playing a tape of soft music. Three people lay under blankets on the carpeted floor. I looked around, wondering what to do next. A young, bearded fellow sensed my dilemma and told me to help myself to a pillow and blanket and find a spot on the floor. I joined the others. The room was so tranquil that I almost dozed off.

At exactly eight o'clock, Gitananda quietly entered the room. In a soothing voice she greeted the students, and for my benefit briefly described the evening. We were going to do postures and breathing exercises and talk about the benefits attained from them. Halfway through the evening, there was a break during which we were treated to herbal tea and apple slices. Peacefully we sat around asking questions of Gitananda. The last hour went even faster than the first.

I continued to go to the ashram every Wednesday evening. I enjoyed it so much, I never missed a lesson. One day Gitananda suggested that I might enjoy spending time with her teacher in India. I had already been hinting that I wanted to go, and the next day I purchased airline tickets. I planned to spend one month in the ashram and two weeks travelling in India.

~

A few weeks later, in the middle of the night, I arrived at the New Delhi airport. There was only one bus outside, and it was completely sold out, the driver said. When I asked him whether he could recommend a hotel, he said his cousin had a very clean hotel and he could arrange a room for me. It would cost only 800 rupees, he said. When I accepted his proposal he told me I could get on the bus after all! Every seat was taken. Even the aisles were packed with passengers. In one corner, the driver gestured that I was to climb on top of the luggage piled almost to the ceiling. It was not a comfortable ride as handles from the luggage poked me in the ribs. With every bump in the road, I hit my head on the ceiling. When we arrived at the hotel, I checked my guide book, which suggested that rates were 250 rupees a night. Not 800 rupees. My benevolent bus driver wasn't so generous after all, I realized, but I was too tired to argue.

Not wanting to be cheated again, I approached the next day with great caution. My next stop was Jaipur, in the state of Rajastan, and I spent the entire morning doing research on bus fares. I was quoted a wide range of prices, from 35 to 500 rupees, then bought a bus ticket for 60 rupees. Proud of my shrewd purchase, I arrived at the bus depot at seven o'clock in the evening, clutching my ticket for seat eight. The bus left on time and I settled in for the night. At the second stop, a man and woman got on the bus and showed me a ticket for seats number seven and eight. They demanded my seat. I refused. Soon everyone in the bus became involved in a shouting match. But I rebuffed any attempt to give up my seat. The atmosphere became very ugly. I was worried they would harm me or even forcibly remove me from the bus. Finally, an official from the terminal interviewed me and promised me a seat on another bus. Reluctantly I got up and surrendered my seat. It was the middle of the night.

I had been waiting for two hours, sitting on a pile of freight at the bus depot, when the official approached and asked if I would ride in the cab of a bus. (In many buses in India, the driver sat up front in a cab or compartment separate from the pasengers and conductor.) He took me to inspect the cab. The front seat had very thin padding, but the cab was roomy. Reluctantly I consented. The other option was to take a refund, but I didn't feel like looking for a hotel this late. We finally got underway. To my surprise, at the next stop two men got into the cab. Ten minutes later, another four were added. I complained to the driver, but he ignored me. A mere hundred yards further, the driver picked up two soldiers carrying shotguns. We were crammed like sardines in the cab. As I was the only non-smoker, I found breathing difficult. The driver was insanely reckless; many times we came within inches of a collision. With that and the constant blowing of the horn, the journey was a nightmare. Finally, we arrived in Jaipur at four o'clock in the morning.

I felt stiff as a board. There was so little circulation left in my legs that I disembarked from the bus with difficulty. At a nearby hotel, a sleepy night clerk eyed me wearily and seemed to take forever to do the registration. While filling out the forms, he was watching the television which was blaring away. Thirty minutes later, he handed me the key to Room 13, which was located on the second floor. The room was large. I looked around, taking in the green chipped paint of the steel bed, the walls streaked with rust-brown water stains, the large holes where plaster had broken off. The tattered bedspread was covered with cigarette burns, and the bedding looked suspect. I decided to sleep in my clothes. I could hear the desk clerk's TV blaring away, but suspected that going downstairs to complain about the volume would be useless. Exhausted, I fell asleep immediately.

After three hours' solid sleep, I got up, splashed cold water on my face in the filthy bathroom, and made a quick exit. Looking for a place to eat breakfast, I tried several hotels, but none appealed. Finally, on one hotel window, I saw a sign offering coffee, and was soon trying to consume the unappetizing coffee, poached eggs, and toast. By now, it was ten o'clock. I took the business card with the name and address of the ashram out of my wallet, and spent the next two hours showing that card to everyone I met, without success. Just as I was about to throw in the towel, a teenage boy took me on the back of his scooter straight to my destination.

The ashram was in a residential district. It looked just like the other residences except it was larger. The only suggestion that this could be an ashram was that the compound was decorated with a few statues of Hindu gods. The number on the card matched the one on the gate, however, so I rang the bell. After a brief pause a man came out of a small building behind the gate and shuffled towards me. He greeted me with the words: "Sai Ram" and opened the gate to let me in. He directed me to an area where shoes and sandals were lined up and said, "Put your shoes over there and I will get the manager." The manager, a young, fair-haired man with a twinkle in his eyes behind gold-rimmed glasses, greeted me and introduced himself as Mukananda. He said that he was from the Netherlands. A Dutchman like me! How could he help me, he asked. I gave him my name, and expected to get some kind of recognition since a fax had been sent to prepare for my arrival. I could tell from the blank look on his face that nothing registered. I explained about the fax. He shook his head and said he hadn't received any communication.

"Why would you want to be here," he asked, "since Swamiji is not expected for several weeks?"

While Mukananda and I were talking, the lunch bell rang and he invited me to join him. "After lunch we will try to figure out what to do with you," he laughed. Over lunch I met the entire population of the ashram — another man from Holland, and three men from Austria, Yugoslavia, and India. The Indian man was the cook and gardener. While we were still eating lunch, a tailor arrived and brought a new outfit for Mukananda. It was made of rough, unbleached cotton. When he tried it on, it was too small. He looked at me and said, "You will need disciple clothes. These might fit you." I tried them on and they did fit perfectly. Eagerly, I made the purchase. I loved the title "disciple" that appeared to come along with the outfit.

After lunch, the Austrian man invited me up on the roof to sit in the sun and chat. I enjoyed listening to his story of transformation, and how he had decided to follow Swamiji. I felt I was in the right place since I too thirsted for changes in my life. In the meantime, I could hear the telephone conversations below as Mukananda tried to solve the problem of what to do with me. At tea-time, Mukananda told me to go to an ashram in Pali, which was also in Rajastan. They would be expecting me, he said. As it was a full day's journey, I would be leaving early in the morning.

My new-found Austrian friend asked the manager if he could accompany me to Pali. The manager thought it an excellent idea and said he would phone Swamiji for permission. After tea we were informed that the Yugoslavian man was to escort me, not the Austrian. The Austrian and I looked at each other with disappointment. By the next day, I still hadn't warmed up to my appointed travelling companion. He was very withdrawn around me, and had no patience with the local people. He spent most of the time growling at them. We took three buses that day. The last one was a Dodge van built to carry eight passengers. Miraculously, it carried thirty. I was crammed into the rear luggage compartment with merchandise of every description. Five other persons were also jammed into that compartment. There was so little room that some of us had more of our bodies outside the bus than inside. This journey was even more painful than the bus ride from New Delhi. This time it wasn't cigarette smoke that bothered me, it was the heavy exhaust fumes from this and other vehicles. Fortunately, it was only an hour-long trip.

We were dropped off on a country road. About half a mile up a dirt path I could see the ashram. It looked impressive sitting in the middle of nowhere, a three-storey white building with pink trim and ornate green-and-red decorations. When we got closer, I noticed two other buildings. One, just slightly to the right, was low-slung with a thatched hay-roof which blended in with the landscape. I learned that it was used as a meeting hall and temple. Just behind that building was a small one which housed the kitchen and had outdoor sinks for washing dishes and brushing teeth and so on. On a platform next to the main building sat a bearded man under an umbrella. He wore an orange robe. My travelling companion acknowledged that it was Swamiji and suggested that I go over and say hello. I was reluctant because I didn't know what to say or do. Besides, I said, Swamiji had an audience and I didn't want to interrupt him.

My companion convinced me that it would be rude not to introduce myself, so I followed his advice. When I was within earshot, I could hear Swamiji talking in Hindi. As soon as he saw me, he switched to English and asked me to sit on the blankets in front of him, alongside his other guests. I was immensely impressed that he was focusing his attention totally on me while the other guests were waiting patiently. For about ten minutes, Swamiji talked with me about my trip and asked about various people from Vancouver. When I felt it was time to leave, he stressed that if I needed anything, I was to see him personally.

After I left Swamiji, I found all one hundred disciples had been given their dinner and were sitting or squatting throughout the ashram. When I asked how to get some food, I was told they had stopped serving, but I might try the kitchen. The cook grumbled about my being late, but when I explained that I had just arrived, he was a little more agreeable. He handed me a tin cup and plate, and told me that I was to clean it after every meal and keep it in my room. I looked for eating utensils, but he told me it would do me good to eat without them. In the corner of the kitchen stood three huge pans of food. A scoop from each was put on my plate. This dinner, as well as every other, consisted of rice, vegetables and dahl (lentil soup). After dinner I was shown to my room by the house-keeping manager. Twelve mats, each about one inch thick, lay on the concrete floor. My guide said, "Take the one in the corner and throw your sleeping bag on it." But I didn't have a sleeping bag! He arranged a "loaner" for me. How many more things could go wrong?

In the evening, I went to the hall for bajans (devotional singing). All the singing was in Sanskrit — to my disappointment, since I enjoyed singing. Even when I saw the words on paper, the music was difficult to follow. After the singing came a question period. One of the questions was: "When will there be a trip to town?" The reply was yes, in two days, on Thursday. Another question was: "Do they sell bottled water in town?" The answer was yes. It was a question I had wanted to ask. I had tried the water at the ashram and spit it out. The strong sulphur taste made it impossible for me to drink. I was looking forward to Thursday when I could buy some water.

Then someone announced that we would be accompanying Swamiji next week to a village where he would be officiating at an opening of a new hospital. Next on the agenda was a talk in English by Swamiji. The topic was how to obtain enlightenment through meditation. I kept nodding off to sleep. After his talk, Swamiji scolded the participants, some for not wearing disciple clothes, others for not fully participating in the ashram activities, and yet others for not surrendering their egos. He told the gathering he knew all this because he could see through his third eye (he pointed to a spot above his nose). After the evening meeting it was time for bed. I tried to talk to some of my roommates and discovered that none spoke English. They all originated from various Slavic countries.

In the morning, a man from Australia was lying on the mat that had been unoccupied the previous evening. I was delighted to have someone to speak with in English. The next few days, I attended all the activities and found myself totally frustrated because the programs were mostly in Sanskrit. Even though all the participants were Westerners, they could sing in Sanskrit as they had learned the chants and songs in their home country beforehand. As agreed, I went to Swamiji and told him about my frustration. He listened attentively and gave me permission to stop attending meetings. He suggested I might enjoy walking around the farm. Also we were going on the road very shortly and that would be fun. Thursday came and went without the much anticipated trip into town. By then, I had found that meal times were changed without notice, or even cancelled, and realized that promised trips fell into the same category. I was becoming more and more frustrated. My Australian roommate and I had developed a very close friendship. He tried to explain the logic for all the changes in the program, and I tried to understand as best as I could.

Most days I wandered in the cultivated lands of the ashram and its neighbours. I spent several hours a day out in the fields, sunbathing in the nude. On Tuesday, after breakfast, two buses and a motorcycle with two police officers arrived. We were told we would be leaving in fifteen minutes for our promised outing! My excitement soared. An hour later, our entourage of four vehicles left the ashram. The first vehicle was the motorcycle with the two police officers, followed by a private passenger vehicle containing Swamiji and his chauffeur. Bringing up the rear were the two buses. After a ninety-minute drive, we came to a village and pulled up in front of the police station. There we disembarked and gathered in the courtyard. Sitting on the ground, we listened to the police chief and Swamiji make speeches in Hindi. Our group of one hundred people from all over the world sang Hindi and Sanskrit songs for the villagers. The feeling of camaraderie was unmistakable. Before we departed on the next leg of our journey, Indian devotees clad in colourful costumes served us tea.

A rattling bus took us to our next destination, which was two hours away — most of it over dirt roads. The floor boards of the ancient bus were pocked with gaping holes which allowed us to see the road underneath. In addition, the dust on the dirt roads created such a particle storm inside the bus that we were gasping for breath. As soon as we arrived at our next stop, we rushed gratefully off the bus, and marshalled outside the village.

The official welcoming committee consisted of a group of men all attired in colourful turbans. The curtains of Swamiji's car had been closed, but when everyone was organized, a signal was given to the chauffeur to open the door. A red carpet was spread in front of the door for Swamiji to walk on. When he emerged from the car, a loud cheer went up and the village men waved their arms exuberantly. A procession was formed, with Swamiji leading the way. The village elders chanted and sang as they took turns putting carpets on the path in front of Swamiji. The ashram group followed. Our entry into the village and our gathering on the grounds of the hospital was a stirring experience. Swamiji was seated on a platform, and was the first speaker. He spoke in Hindi. About a dozen other people also delivered speeches, speaker after speaker droning on in Hindi. After two hours of sitting on the hard ground, I was in agony with pain in my legs and buttocks. Patience truly is a virtue I can practise now, I thought.

Before we entertained the crowd with singing, Swamiji explained that the speakers had told the story of extreme hardship in the village and the surrounding farms, for they hadn't had rain in five years. One of the reasons they had invited Swamiji was for him to produce rain. He asked us whether he should grant their request. Most people in the ashram group shouted, "Yes!" I was silent. I felt nauseated by Swamiji's boastfulness; I didn't believe he had the capability to perform miracles. Meanwhile Swamiji told a story about a farmer who had shot an animal and cooked it for supper. When this vegetarian community heard of the farmer's deed, they all began a one-day fast. Upon hearing this story, the ashram group responded with applause. Again, I was out of step with the group. My sympathy lay with the farmer when food was so scarce.

The village community showered Swamiji with gifts, including a rug, blankets, and a sizeable roll of rupee notes. After this the men of the village served us a delicious lunch. I was impressed — even overwhelmed — by the hospitality of these people. They apparently had so little to give and yet were such extraordinary hosts. Wistfully I left them behind as we boarded buses again. After a forty-five-minute ride, we disembarked at yet another village and crammed into the narrow main street. I resigned myself to more speeches, but fortunately the microphone wasn't working and all we got was one short speech from a disgruntled Swamiji. By the time we climbed back on the bus, it was dusk. On the ride home, I was pleasantly tired but fulfilled. This day had been exciting. When I crawled into my sleeping bag that evening, for the first time I didn't notice the hardness of the concrete floor, but immediately fell into a sound sleep.

The next day I was summoned to the office to discuss payment for my stay. In Vancouver, I had been told that the stay in the ashram would be 45 rupees a day, which is about U.S. $2. Considering the minimal quality of the food and accommodation, that seemed to be about right. I wasn't expecting to be asked for U.S. $36 a day when I arrived at the office. I didn't have anything close to that amount of money with me and settled the account with a personal cheque.

At the next day's meeting, we were told that we would go into Pali (the town) the following day. At last I would able to buy bottled water, and satisfy my craving for a chocolate bar! But the next morning the trip to Pali was cancelled again. Furthermore, that day lunch was served at eleven o'clock, even though it had always been served at noon. When I returned from a walk, lunch was over, and since I was late, I wasn't allowed to have any. I was getting angry. I sought out my friend, Arbu from Australia, and told him I'd had enough; I was leaving. First he tried to convince me that these frustrations were good for me. He said I was too attached to routine and objects, and the ashram was doing me favour. When he didn't succeed in convincing me, he suggested that I go to see Swamiji.

I accepted the latter and went upstairs to Swamiji's quarters. There I was told that he couldn't see me. I fumed under my breath, then spent the rest of the day trying to decide on my next course of action. The questions I tried to deal with were: Why am I here? Is this man indeed a Divine Light? Is this stay worth $36 a day? The answer to my first question was quite revealing. I discovered that it was my secret wish to become a Divine Light myself. I could see myself going home as a dignified swami, wearing disciple clothes and feeling superior. It was a shock to discover how much I longed for recognition. And was this holy man indeed a Divine Light? What did that look like? The answer to that I didn't know with certainty, but a gnawing feeling told me that I was not in the right place. I knew that I was no longer learning from this experience, but didn't know what to do about it.

That evening I had a long conversation with Arbu again, with nothing resolved. Breakfast the next morning consisted of a bland mush that looked like creamed rice. As I gazed at it, I realized that it was time to move on. I said good-bye to Arbu and went upstairs to pack my bag, feeling very sure of my decision. While I was walking towards the main road, I almost expected to be zapped by

Swamiji, but obviously I gave him more power than he had. Once I got to the road I realized I didn't know how to get to Pali or where I would be going after that. While I was considering a number of options, a mini-bus came up the road. I flagged it down, and to my relief, it was heading for Pali. I was headed into town at last!

Chapter 9

~

Vipassana

In 1994, I tried again to learn meditation. I had talked to people who could meditate, and from what they described, it was the art of *listening* to God, rather than talking to God, in prayer. I wanted to learn to do that.

At that time, I was a frequent visitor at St. Joseph drug and alcohol treatment centre in Calcutta. One day there, I was having lunch with Father John and the subject got around to meditation. I shared that the art of meditation had been very elusive for me. Father John recommended the ancient Buddhist method of meditation called Vipassana. He assured me that if I should lose my Roman Catholic beliefs as a result, he would re-install them. I thanked him for his concern, but told him that I was not a Roman Catholic and that would not be necessary.

The next day I went in search of the address he had given me, and found it in an import-export office after many hours of looking. I was served tea and handed two pages of instruction about the Vipassana retreat. The instructions included the requirement to observe rigorously the following five precepts:

To abstain from killing.

To abstain from stealing.

To abstain from all sexual activities.

To abstain from telling lies.

To abstain from all intoxicants.

I signed up for the next course. In the meantime, I met several people who had attended Vipassana meditation previously. They talked about how they, or others, had got in touch with themselves. They also described people freaking out while doing the meditating, and that I found frightening. However, to get in touch with myself, and to get some insight into my inner workings, was something I was thirsting for. After my usual struggle with the transportation system, I arrived at the Vipassana ashram in northern Calcutta.

~

The Vipassana ashram was located on the banks of the Hooghly River. The building looked like a palace, and perhaps had been the home of an Indian prince or dignitary. The first day of the retreat was the only day we were allowed outside the gate. I took advantage of that to sit on the river bank along with a few hundred neighbourhood people who were either bathing in the river or watching the sunset like myself.

The next day was the first of ten days of silence. My room contained twelve men; all but two of us were from India. The bed was a small bunk padded with a horsehair mattress and covered with a mosquito net. I found sleep difficult that night. The mattress was uncomfortable, one man in the room was snoring loudly, and there was a horde of mosquitoes buzzing outside my net. Upon waking at the required 4:00 a.m., however, I heard only silence.

The first meditation began at 4:30 a.m. When I arrived at the meditation room, some space was available against the wall, but I chose a spot in the middle of the room. Unfortunately, I didn't realize that this was to be my permanent location for the entire course, and I soon regretted my choice. Within half an hour, I was in agony without back support. My buttocks were especially uncomfortable on the thin cushion. Each day started at 4 a.m. and ended at 9:30 p.m., and each day I spent in that position was agony.

I feigned illness for a few days to get a reprieve from the sitting. While I was in bed, one of the assistants, a kind and concerned older man, fussed over me. He brought me fruit and yogurt, which was a welcome relief from our usual diet of curried vegetables and rice. Another challenge was the army of mosquitoes, which were plentiful and extremely active. We were not allowed to kill — and that included mosquitoes. Applying lotion gave me some relief from the bites, but a few did get killed by my wrath, and I feared I might be punished by God, Buddha, or ashram officials. At the end of the ten days, we were encouraged to make a donation since the course itself did not have a fixed fee. The homework was that we would do two thirty-minute sessions of meditation a day once we returned home.

I have not followed through with even one meditation session. I started the Vipassana course with high hopes for a breakthrough in my ability to meditate, but failed again.

Nowadays I have given up the thirst to be a meditator, and at the same time have given up the need to punish myself for not succeeding. The lesson I have learned was not to be to attached to the results. Had I been more relaxed, or been able to maintain the sitting posture, what would have been the result? I do seem to have better results while being active — for example, sometimes I am able to meditate while driving a car or working in a garden. Since meditation has been so elusive for me, I have adopted the philosophy that if it's meant to be, it will be. If it's not meant to be, I will accept that too.

Chapter 10

~

Osho

Christianity and all other religions are part of the
conspiracy to castrate man. They have destroyed
all the dignity of man, they have given him only
guilt and sin. Hence I call Christianity the
deadliest poison.

– Osho Rajneesh (from *Christianity and Zen,*
The Rebel Publishing House, Cologne, Germany, 1989)

I first heard of Osho and his controversial ashram while
waiting for a flight home after my third trip to India. I was
in the departure lounge at Calcutta's airport and was
lounging on the concrete floor with my head resting on
my backpack since all the chairs were taken with luggage,
coats and sweaters. I was lying there watching with good
humour the other passengers. As ever, I was amazed with
how the Indians travel. They seem to carry everything
with them but the kitchen sink! The trip had been
pleasant; I was feeling contented and was already
contemplating my next trip to India. Two young
American women threw their backpacks on the floor next

to me, and headed for the toilet. I instantly became the custodian of their possessions.

There is an unwritten code amongst backpackers that we look after each other. We also establish bonds easily. Generally we don't relate as well to those in business suits — *they* look well groomed, *we* look scruffy. When we backpackers first meet, the conversations are based on questions like: Where are you from? Where are you going? Where have you been? In that way, I discovered that these young women had been to the Osho ashram in Pune. In fact, they and ten thousand others had spent Christmas there. The ashram did not sound like any I had visited. I was decidedly intrigued when they talked about the exciting workshops they had taken. The courses were on personal relationships, self improvement, yoga, art, and even tennis. I promised myself to include Pune in my next visit to India.

When I got back home, I made inquiries about Osho, the founder of the ashram. Although now I have read four books written by Osho and two books about him, at that time I couldn't find much information. I did learn that Osho was a new name; his old names had been Rajneesh and Bhagwan. At one time he had had an ashram in the state of Oregon, and that ashram was famous for drugs and sex. He had been deported from the United States, founded a new ashram in India, and died there in 1990. I personally had no interest in drugs, but I was curious about the sex programs. Did they have orgies? Did they teach you how to have orgies? Or did they take a spiritual approach to sex? An acquaintance said that he had been to the ashrams in India and the United States ten times. He felt sure that I would enjoy the ashram. He said it was a great place to learn to love, and of course I wanted to learn to love. Eight months later, in the spring of 1995, I went to Pune to investigate the Osho ashram for myself.

~

I was astounded by the exquisite beauty of the ashram. Exceedingly clean and cared for, the tree-lined street leading to the ashram was like no other I had seen in India. Even the adjoining houses, hotel, and hospital were well maintained and the grounds were manicured and spotless. In the middle of the block were two gates, one on each side of the road. Between these gates, a constant stream of people on foot crossed the road. Most were women and almost all wore clinging maroon robes. Each flashed photo identification at the gate guards. The main gate was on the right. Next to it was an impressive waterfall cascading down the an ornate concrete wall into a sparkling pool. Next to the gate was an elaborately furnished outdoor reception area. I decided to investigate.

I sauntered up to a desk which had a sign on it. Applications, the sign said. While I was deciding what to say to the man at the desk, he initiated conversation by welcoming me. Like the women I had seen, he wore a maroon robe. Warmth exuded from him. In a jovial Irish brogue, he asked me a few questions. Had I been here before? Why did I come? Where did I live? He summed up by giving me a stern lecture on my expected behaviour if I joined the ashram — for instance, no drugs or alcohol. Then he handed me a form to complete. When I returned the completed form, I was directed to another desk. AIDS Tests, this sign said. There I discovered that no one was permitted to enter the ashram without an AIDS test. I was told to come back after four hours to get the test results. If they were negative, I would receive my photo ID pass.

Having four hours free, I relocated my belongings from downtown Pune to Kerogan Park to be closer to the ashram. The ashram itself did not have accommodation. I was fortunate to get a room only one hundred metres away. I also purchased a maroon robe, which was required for most of the activities.

My test results were favourable and I was issued a pass. That evening I ate dinner in one of the four ashram restaurants. The food was a delicious vegetarian buffet. After dinner I was asked to leave the grounds since I did not have a white robe. I was a bit miffed since no one had until then alluded to the need for a white robe. I was told that every evening a phenomenon called "the White Robe Brotherhood" transpired, and admission was by white robe only. Participants were also required to bathe or shower without scented soap or perfume. At the entrance to the hall, "sniffer crews" were stationed to enforce this directive. Apparently Osho had been very sensitive to smells. Anyone passing the smell test then had to pass through a metal detector. (I never found out the reason for the metal detectors.) Those suffering with a cough or sniffles went to a separate room equipped with closed-circuit TV monitors.

The White Robe Brotherhood was held in the spacious Buddha hall, which could hold ten thousand participants. The focus of the hall was on an empty chair formerly used by Osho. Most believed that he was still present, that he had only discarded his body. The nightly discourse by Osho was presented using videos which had been taped years before, with a live band helping to create the mood before and after the videos. A portion of the evenings included the band stimulating the audience of thousands to a feverish pitch. The hall exploded with shouts of "Osho, Osho, Osho!" I found the atmosphere hysterical and resisted participation.

My reaction to the videos ranged from disgust, interest, humour, fear, and indifference. At times Osho would launch vicious attacks on Mother Teresa, Jesus Christ, President Reagan or almost anyone else. No one was exempt. He loved to be controversial. At other times he would poke fun at himself or others. Sometimes I found him profound; at other times, boring. When he went on a verbal rampage, it was made clear that the audience should applaud and cheer wildly. Whenever this happened, I cringed. I felt that the participants were being hypnotized by a skilful manipulator.

On that first day in Pune, I went back to the ashram after the white robe event was finished and joined others in the dance that followed. Everyone danced without partners. To me, the dances were liberating and fun and a great way to unwind. After the dance I explored some of the complex. Tucked away in a corner I found a bar (serving real booze). I ordered a soft drink and joined a table of eight. A helpful German woman sitting at the table was a fount of information on both the ashram and Pune. She also lent me a white robe for my week's stay at the ashram. Happy and contented, I left the bar at closing and retreated to my room.

I spent the entire next day exploring all four sections of the ashram grounds. What a place! Behind the ashram was a public park donated to the city by Osho. A creek coursed through the middle, full of tiny waterfalls and ponds created by damming and excavating. The park designer had effectively used the shrubs, water, and rocks to create an atmosphere conducive to quiet reflection. Paths led to secluded benches, an aviary, and a variety of statues.

Adjoining the park was the newest section of the compound. The buildings were constructed of black and white marble and were in the shape of pyramids. The upper levels accommodated classrooms and the lower floors contained washrooms, showers, and hundreds of rental lockers, all of which were shared by men and women alike. I was often challenged to be nonchalant around nude female bodies. The main section of the compound consisted of the Buddha hall, restaurants, book shop, kitchen, swimming pool, tennis courts, offices, classrooms, bar, and Osho's former residence, which was now a shrine. It was also the home of a Rolls Royce limousine, one of ninety-three Osho used to own. The fourth area had restaurants as well as a theatre, and workshops for painting, sculpting, acting, music, dance, and photography. In addition, the ashram had a medical clinic, post office, travel agency, and telephone office. My guess was that the ashram was about fifty acres in size. Careful planning had obviously gone into creating a paradise with a luxurious ambience of well-being.

My last day in Pune, I met my friend who was there for his eleventh visit. With his expertise, I finally understood what my expectations could be at the ashram. I had been talking with a woman named Michelle when my friend arrived. After she left he said, "Did you notice how interested she was in you?" I said, "No." He explained that the reason most people were there was for enlightenment through sex. I was dumbfounded that I hadn't discovered it myself! That night, as we had dinner together, my friend went into detail about his own sexual encounters at the ashram, which were many since there was an abundance of willing partners. I felt rather stupid not recognizing the messages I had been getting from Michelle. Also, all week I hadn't grasped the hints from my neighbour, Lois. I was unhappy about this being my last day, but I knew I would be back.

~

Back in Vancouver, while leafing through a magazine, I noticed an ad about an "Osho Tantra" group. Wanting to learn more, I enrolled. I soon learned that in the meetings it was compulsory to share exactly what you wanted to say. An example: I told Jane she was nice. Keith, the group leader, stated: "You want to fuck her!" I protested: "That's not what I said." Keith responded: "But you do want to fuck her? Ask her if she wants to fuck." By this time I was totally embarrassed and wanted to escape, but the group, including Jane, encouraged me to ask the question. After protesting some more, I finally agreed to go along. The group was sitting on the floor in a circle. Jane and I were told to sit in the centre facing each other. Reluctantly, I blurted out: "Do you want to fuck?" She said: "No!"

I howled with laughter. What a relief! The aim of that practice was to say clearly what you want, both of you. The moral was that the truth never hurts. It started me thinking. I realized that when Jane refused my offer, I did not feel rejected. Halfway through the evening Keith asked the group: "How are we doing? Are we going too fast, or too slow?" Saul, a man in his twenties, said: "I want to take my clothes off." Keith said, "Do you want music?" Saul said that he did. Keith turned on the CD player, and Saul got up and started dancing.

Again I was asking myself, What am I doing here? After Saul was fully nude, he danced in my direction and said, "Touch me," indicating his penis. I covered my head with my arms and tried to ignore him. Again the group urged me to do something, and I finally yelled out: "Fuck off!" Saul said, "OK." Again I roared with laughter. It felt so liberating to get straight answers! After Saul's dance, Sheila urgently wanted to talk about her failing relationship with her husband. When she said, "I would like to take my blouse off," Keith said, "Go ahead." Sheila said, "I can't; my husband would not approve." After a long period of everyone assessing whether she should or shouldn't, she came to the conclusion that one of the reasons her relationship didn't work was that she allowed her husband to dictate her lifestyle. To defy him, she took her blouse off. We all congratulated her on her courage. I suspected this may have been a major breakthrough for her. At the conclusion of evening, although she was still undecided as to whether she would tell her husband, the look of confidence on her face demonstrated her new fortitude.

These meetings were challenging and confrontational, and included coarse language and nudity. I spent a lot of time reacting and judging, but knew that buttons I had thought were comatose were being pushed within me. Even though I disliked parts of the encounters, I knew I wanted to pursue more of this alternate approach.

∾

That winter of 1995, I returned to India for the fifth time. I planned to stay four months — two in Pune, and two in Calcutta. I arrived full of expectations, anticipating finally learning how to have successful relationships. In Pune, I paid a month's rent on a garden apartment, a bicycle, and a locker at the ashram. I came prepared to do the work required to attain my goals, and to indulge in the social as well as the spiritual events at the ashram. I wanted to make contact with people, particularly with women. I registered for four courses, the first of which was Self Love. It was recommended as an introduction to the ashram. I found that it offered me little new information. I was gratified to confirm that my love of self was OK. Just to be sure I wasn't deluding myself, I asked the instructor for a conference. We agreed that I had dealt with most of my resentments and had been successful in self-forgiveness.

I met many people in that group, but Helmut and I spent a lot of time together in lunch and coffee breaks. He and his wife were staunch followers of Osho. As emancipated spirits, they had agreed to release the shackles from each other and were free to sleep with whomever they desired. When I first met Helmut, his glum look told me that something was wrong. Later, when he had gained confidence in me, his story came to light. The previous evening his wife had brought home a new lover and occupied the bedroom next to his. I asked him why he didn't do the same. He said he was feeling so much pain that he didn't feel like it; furthermore, he loved his wife a great deal. Daily he would supply an update on her latest lover, as she had a different one each night. My heart went out to him in his pain.

As for me, I was open to having female companionship, but found myself totally frustrated by the response to my overtures. For instance, early in my stay I met a woman called Barbara. We got along exceedingly well. One day after we had been to dinner, I suggested we go to my place. She accepted — eagerly, I thought. In the dark beside the pool, we sat in a swing couch, rocking back and forth. I was aware that rats lived in the area and Barbara too soon discovered the furry little animals running around the pool. For a while she was quite brave as they came closer and closer, but finally she decided it was time to go home. We climbed on our bicycles and pedalled to her house. She had roommates — that ended any chances for intimacy that night.

The following evening, we had dinner again. Practising what I had learned in Vancouver and in the Osho group, I suggested we become intimate later. She said that she was taken aback by my proposition, and that the answer was no. She told me she had never had a normal relationship with a man, that just thinking of sex would make her freeze up. For three weeks, we did a lot of cycling and had a few dinners. Her experiences in her ashram groups included men making passes at her. As a result, she kept going deeper and deeper into depression. Twice she arrived at my room in the middle of the night to tell me her latest tale of woe. She was losing her composure and I feared she might harm herself. Two times when I saw her approaching I did a quick detour to avoid her, but most of the time I was there to support her since nothing exciting was happening in my life.

The second program was on hurtful past relationships. Again it was an area where I had done extensive work, and I found it of limited value. Even so, I learned some wonderful new healing tools, and met a number of interesting people. In this course, I was attracted to Anna, three years my junior. She told me she had spent all her life being sheltered by her parents. With difficulty she had managed to separate herself from them for a few weeks to go to Pune. She was experiencing great joy in her dedication to Osho. She never missed a discourse or a meditation. I believed that had the ashram told her to drink poison, she would gladly have done so for Osho. To obtain enlightenment in a three-week vacation was hard work, and Anna found the twelve-hour days exhausting. Every decision she made was prefaced by: What would Osho do? Her frantic search resulted in extreme mood swings with the lows getting lower each day. In the seven days I was acquainted with her, she changed accommodation eight times. Finally she released herself from the treadmill she was on, and flew home two weeks early, disillusioned. Was this an extreme case of gullibility? Unfortunately, it was not. Another woman I was spending time with was Ingrid. She too was looking for Osho to lead her out of the wilderness, but confided that it wasn't succeeding.

One evening the subject of Osho's discourse was: "Expectations lead to frustration." That was the message that I needed to hear for myself. That explained why I was feeling frustrated — I did have all kinds of expectations and they weren't being fulfilled. A huge burden was lifted from my shoulders. The next day I told Ingrid how thrilled I was to learn of the formula: "Expectation equals frustration." Her response was that she had gone there expecting Osho to show her the way to live, and she would settle for nothing less. A week later she fell apart at the seams, and she, too, left the ashram early. Devastated, she went home to pick up the pieces and reconstruct her life. She told me she had had enough of "this phoney Osho." She was going back to Germany to join the Sai Baba group, where she was sure she would find what she was looking for.

In the third workshop, I earned a first degree in Reiki, the art of healing touch. I hadn't been impressed with Reiki as a way of healing, but my experience in this four-day course changed my mind. I looked forward to each day of the course and witnessed some major shifts both as a recipient and as an administrator of Reiki. I was told numerous times that I had good hands, and unfortunately started to believe it. My challenge was to acknowledge that it had nothing to do with me — I was only a channel of the greater power.

In this group, I met two other Canadians. Allen and his wife were staying for six months. At Osho's suggestion, they said, they were going to break out of the bondage that comes with being married. Being good devotees, they decided to follow Osho's advice and sleep with others. Two weeks later, Allen's wife found a lover and moved in with him, only coming home twice to pick up some clothes. Allen was in shock, but tried to persuade me, and himself, that this way was best since Osho had said so. After the wife's lover flew home to England, she returned home to Allen, and he was ecstatic. A day later, however, she moved in with someone else. Allen kept assuring me that Osho knew what he was talking about, and this was the best contract. In the meantime, he had stopped eating and lost twenty pounds, and was in great emotional pain. He would never admit that this experiment was a failure. When I left Pune, Allen took over my apartment. By that time, he had left his wife. (A year later I ran into him at a meeting, where he was guru shopping.)

I had intended staying in Pune for two months, but after two weeks I wanted to leave. Since I had paid the rent on the apartment, bicycle and locker, I decided to stay, but no longer went to the ashram daily. Instead, I attended twelve-step meetings and went for long bicycle rides. My social life switched from the ashram to the twelve-step group, where we had birthday parties, lunches and dinners. It was a fun group.

During this time, reading books became my passion. I had acquired a number of books written by Osho, and enjoyed them. To my surprise, most of what he wrote made sense to me. Then why was there all this unhappiness around his ashram? His anti-establishment views were attracting those who had been had been hurt by officialdom such as the church and the state. His way of thinking, however, seemed to suggest throwing the baby out with the bath water, and the results created a good deal of pain. In my hotel I saw two people lose it. Flip out! I often heard the woman next door groan until one day she disappeared. Her clothes were left in the room and when I checked out ten days later she still hadn't been heard from. The hotel manager said this was a common occurrence. Another woman had been banned from the ashram for being unstable, and the hotel manager tried to cope with her irrational behaviour. Finally, out of despair, he phoned the German consulate to arrange for her to be shipped home. I was told that several times a year the German consulate came to the rescue of its citizens in Pune. The ashram's attitude was that it was not a hospital — when an unstable person mentally collapsed, the ashram simply banned the person from the ashram.

My last two weeks in Pune, I took most of my meals in a restaurant called the German Bakery. Most of its clients were ashram dropouts. All day I would hear the stories of disillusioned devotees. It was hard not to become totally crestfallen. A common complaint was that the ashram promised enlightenment through meditation. The ashram claimed that there were several ways to meditate, including gardening, scrubbing floors, peeling potatoes, and washing dishes, to name a few. In addition, meditation was held in the large Buddha hall five times a day, and pressure was applied to attend all of those sessions. Most of those meditations were with movement, such as jumping, dancing, shaking, singing, and shouting. I had never before heard of this type of meditation. I wondered whether again I was being too critical.

I knew that my primary thirst was to establish a relationship, but I had to admit that I also wanted to indulge in lots of sex. That didn't seem to me to be a very noble purpose. It was true that the fourth program, on tantra (sexual energy), was the main reason I had returned to Pune. In the pre-registration interview required prior to joining the group, I had difficulty convincing the leaders that I was open enough to participate. Eventually, they allowed me in. The group consisted of ten men and ten women. (Since most of the course involved partners, even numbers were required.)

The opening exercise was to sit in front of each other, man to woman, for ten minutes and make eye contact. With four women, my experience was a total failure — they kept looking away and breaking the contact. With three others, the results were OK. With the remaining three, it was magic. Looking deeply into their eyes, I felt as if I could see their inner souls, their beauty, their compassion, their love for me, and mine for them. This experience was not sexual. At the end of the day, two of these three women shared with me how profound the experience had been for them. I said that for me, too, it had been a soul-rendering encounter.

Each session was started by a dance. While dancing, each person chose a partner for the morning or afternoon. We were required to have a new partner each time. I was always the last to be selected, maybe because I was the oldest, had more wrinkles than anyone, and was almost bald. My self-worth was taking a beating. I had many reluctant partners, and after three days, I was wanting out. At the beginning of the group, however, we had all made a contract to stay for the entire five days.

Each of the daily exercises involved a considerable amount of hugging and touching, often under blankets and semi-nude. (We were required to wear underpants and to keep them on.) On the afternoon of the second to last day, my partner refused to participate in an exercise which necessitated lying close together and breathing in unison. A requirement at the end of each session was to spend some time talking about the episode. My partner was the first to share. She told me that this was the worst experience she had had at the ashram. I was dumbfounded. I wanted to scream, but instead retaliated by declaring that I thought she had a major problem. My accusation was met with even more abuse. I apologized. That night I was in much emotional pain, and ran this event through my mind over and over. The conclusion I reached was that it was not the rejection that was the problem, but my desperate need to be loved. Then I remembered that recently I had heard a speaker expound: "No one can reject you. It is impossible." I didn't agree at the time, but now in desperation I was willing to put it to the test.

The next day, I resolved that during the dance I would ask someone to partner with me rather than the other way around. I was going to make my selection on the basis of not the easiest partner, but the most difficult. The woman I picked didn't have the courage to say no, but showed her disgust and contempt by scowling. To my amazement, I was enjoying the rejection. She resolved not to participate, while I resolved to follow the instructions with or without her help. I stayed focused on my partner with complete love. At the end of the session, I was the first to share our experience. Without sarcasm I told her it was a great experience, even though she had seemed a little reluctant. She exploded into a tirade which included questioning my sanity. For her it had been horrible, she said. I smiled, and she gave me a disgusted look.

That afternoon session was our last. Before we went into the dance, we did some sharing. One woman said that men were creeps, and the world was fucked up. When the music started she didn't get up to join in, but stayed on the floor sulking. I joined her on the floor. She begged me to leave her alone and find someone else, but I stayed there responding only with loving energy. Often throughout the session, she went into hysterics followed by sobbing. I felt whole, grounded, and healed. I didn't need her to love me. I didn't feel pity or self-righteousness. I felt only love. In the weeks that followed, we became trusting friends.

This last Osho group was my greatest teacher. I had started it looking for a relationship and sex, but what I found was something much better. I received a whole new slant on patience, understanding, love, and giving up on expectations.

Chapter 11

~

Miracles in Chamba

While I have not adopted the philosophy of any one guru, I can say that I have found many miracle-workers in India. Among them are those who donate their time, money, and energy to serve the poor. For example, I have been privileged to work in two different operating rooms with five different doctors — one from Bihar and four from New Delhi. They all donate their time to Mother Teresa's leprosy hospitals. Twice a year, in addition to their regular time as volunteers, they organize seven to ten days of mobile surgery in the Himalayan foothills. To attract patients, they put up posters saying that the patients will receive free medical help or surgery. Using a school or tent as a base, the doctors expect to treat about five thousand people per trip. Each of these trips costs the doctors a total of between $3,000 and $5,000, which includes all expenses, even medicines — quite a bargain at less than $1 U.S. per patient. This chapter is about my most recent experience at one of these camps.

~

My arrival time in New Delhi was usually around three o'clock in the morning, and this trip in early October 1997 was no exception. My first challenge was to arrive safely at my preferred district and hotel. The street that I chose to live on was called "the Main Bazaar." That sounded impressive, but it was actually a very narrow road, and at three in the morning had virtually no lights. At the beginning of the street, I took a deep breath, then gathered up my courage and walked down the middle of the road. There was no traffic at that hour, and the rats mostly scurried close to the buildings rather than in the street. Walking in the middle of the road also gave me a better vantage point to be aware not only of attackers, but also of touts from the hotels and taxi drivers, much the more frequent problem. Suddenly, a man appeared from the shadows. I almost jumped out of my skin. Luckily, he was a tout for a local hotel. I admitted that I didn't have a hotel reservation (I didn't need one where I was staying), and he followed me, urging me to stay at a certain hotel. I knew that this was his way of trying to make a commission, but it seemed a very long three blocks to my hotel.

By the time I reached my hotel, twenty-six hours had elapsed since I left my home in Vancouver. I had slept only about two hours in that time, but my time clock was so out of sync that I managed only four hours' sleep at the hotel. After breakfast, I ventured out into the street where merchants were busy unlocking their shop doors and hauling display tables out onto the road. Tea stalls were filled to capacity with early morning customers. Some were reading newspapers; others were blissfully staring out into space as they sipped tea.

Even blindfolded, I would have known that I was in New Delhi. Far from being colourless and odourless, the air was so thick that it seemed to have substance. My initial question to myself when I breathed this air was always the same: What am I doing here? As always, the tea-sippers answered my question. What I experienced over my many visits to India was a bliss similar to what appeared to be happening in this early-morning scene in the main bazaar in New Delhi. I could never get enough.

It was the first time I was in India in response to a special invitation. Two weeks before, I had received a letter from Dr. S. Chada inviting me to join two medical camps he and his colleagues had planned. The first was scheduled for Chamba in the state of Himachal Pradesh, and the other six weeks later in the state of Bihar. During a previous trip to New Delhi, I had indicated to Dr. Chada that I would like to join him and his team in one of their semi-annual free medical camps. When I received these two invitations, I was exhilarated. I had worked with most of these doctors in both New Delhi and Shanti Nagar. Now I was to get an opportunity to travel with them, to expand the scope and the variety of my exposure to medical procedures . . . and once again, to see miracle-workers in action.

From my hotel, I tried to reach Dr. Chada by phone without success. Since I had his address, I decided to present myself in person. As usual, I struggled with the transportation system, and spent a frustrating four hours getting to my destination. (The return trip took only forty-five minutes.) The street in front of the clinic was full of deep ruts and there were piles of garbage everywhere. The exterior looked like a warehouse, but a faded sign above the door announced Dr. Chada's clinic. About fifty people were milling around a door on the right. On the left, a well-dressed woman was sitting at a desk stacked with papers. She spotted me, and said, "Come with me." She elbowed her way through the crowd and I followed. We went through the doorway that everyone one else was trying to enter.

Dr. Chada was sitting at a small desk in the middle of the room. When he saw me, he jumped up and greeted me with an enthusiastic hand shake. He asked me to sit down. Around the room ten people were sitting or standing as they waited their turn to see the doctor. In one corner of the windowless room was a curtained-off area. I could see a pair of feet under the curtain. Abruptly the curtain was slid open to reveal a patient reclining on an examination table, his stomach exposed. Another man came from behind the curtain and spoke a few words to Dr. Chada in Hindi. Dr. Chada excused himself, went to the patient, put his stethoscope on the man's stomach, and nodded in agreement. Then he came back to me.

While we talked, staff came in and asked questions which received either a yes or a no or a brief reply such as "Give him 5 c.c. of ———" or "Test the urine." I never felt that I was being ignored. Dr. Chada seemed to have the uncanny ability to do several things at one time. Just the same, I felt very uncomfortable about taking up the time of such an extremely busy person and cut my social visit short.

He showed me the facility, which included an operating theatre and six beds for patients. There was a staff of six people — two junior doctors, three nurses, and an office manager. The clinic processed five hundred patients a day and Dr. Chada interviewed each and every one of them. One reason Dr. Chada's clinic was packed to capacity was the fees — the suggested charge per visit was only 10 rupees. Some paid more, some paid less, depending on depending on the type of consultation and the ability to pay. The clinic rarely referred patients elsewhere; if surgery was needed, it was performed right there on the premises by Dr. Chada. His average working day was twelve hours, except Wednesday when he volunteered at the Missionaries of Charity leprosy centre in New Delhi.

The next day a group composed of nine doctors, their families, and me boarded a night train to Pathankot in the Punjab. We arrived in the early morning, and were to meet our bus. When our bus did not show, I was told to stand in front of the group, since the bus driver had been told to look for twenty-three Indians and one white man. So I stood in the road and waited for the bus. Forty-five minutes later, a man arrived on a scooter and told us to follow him since breakfast had been arranged at a nearby house. As always, I just carried a light backpack, but most of the others struggled with heavy suitcases. Finally, four rickshaws were recruited to carry the luggage. It was less than a kilometre's walk to our destination.

We arrived at large two-storey house, and were served a delicious breakfast of many vegetarian delicacies. In addition to the servants of the house bringing us the food, the hostess of the house had also recruited some of her neighbours to assist. This meal had been arranged by the female guru who was in part sponsoring the trip. She had several ashrams throughout India.

Totally satisfied, we boarded the bus, which had arrived while we ate. One by one, the people with whom I hadn't visited during the train ride or over breakfast came and sat with me in the bus and introduced themselves. We spent the bus journey talking, singing, eating, and laughing. I was glad to be distracted from the road, which was narrow and steep. The large bus had trouble negotiating some curves and sometimes would have to back up and go forward several times to complete a turn. By mid-afternoon, we reached the former British hill station of Dalhousie, and disembarked at a Hindu temple where we were to sleep that evening.

After the long bus ride, most of us were anxious to exercise. Some went for a walk; others shopped in the town. Then we all met in a local restaurant for our evening meal. The food was very good and the chatter delightful. Most of us retreated to our rooms early since we had had a full and rewarding day. After breakfast the next day, we boarded the bus again for our final destination: Chamba. This day's journey was mostly downhill, and in early afternoon we arrived in the Chamba Valley. Someone in the group told me that because of its mountains, Chamba was called the Switzerland of India.

For the next few days, I shared a room with five doctors. We were billeted in a house next to the ashram where the medical camp would be held. After settling in, I went and explored the surrounding area. Another bus had arrived two days earlier with nursing staff as well as all of our equipment. I joined in on a tour of the facilities. After that, I gave myself a tour of the charming town a kilometre from the ashram.

∾

I was on duty at the O.T. (operating theatre) desk when a woman appeared carrying a bundled-up baby. The woman was on the verge of tears. She handed her bundle to my colleague, who indicated that he didn't want the blanket or the clothes, only the baby. When I saw the baby without her clothes, I was shocked. The baby, whose name was Choti, had been born with a large tumour attached to her hip. She weighed about five pounds; the tumour weighed about three. Her most immediate problem was the tumour was robbing her of the nutrients needed for her development. Another problem was that if the tumour was not removed and continued to grow at its present rate, Choti would find it difficult, if not impossible, to move around.

When Choti was taken away for surgery, the woman started to cry, and so did I. I tried to be brave and told her the doctors were the best and not to worry, but soon discovered she didn't understand English at all. For the next ninety minutes, however, we managed to communicate without a word being spoken. Sometimes we prayed; sometimes we just smiled at each other; other times we cried. Both of us were emotionally exhausted when we heard a baby's cry from inside the operating room. Choti was still alive!

A few minutes later, an attendant came out of the O.T. carrying something wrapped in green surgical cloth. He opened the cloth and showed us the tumour. I asked him where the baby was and he said she was in the recovery room. I asked whether the woman and I could see her, and he said yes. I went in and the woman followed. When we saw the small bundle lying on the bed, I knew I was part of a miracle. Again, the woman and I both wept, this time for joy.

Every day I visited the recovery ward to visit Choti, and gradually, with the help of the translators, I heard the story of how she had come there. After Choti was born, her mother, Chenu, and her grandmother, Zari, took her to the local village dispensary in the village of Samber. The baby's father, Dilip Kumar, had to stay home to work in the family's rice fields. The dispensary staff were sympathetic to Choti's dilemma, but didn't have the expertise to remove the tumour. They told Chenu and Zari not to delay in having the tumour removed, since it was taking nutrients required for the development of the baby's body and brain. The clinic recommended that they go to the hospital twenty kilometres away in Chamba where there were facilities to perform such an operation.

Since the landlord had threatened to evict them if he didn't soon receive his half of their meagre crop, Chenu and Dilip had to work in the fields to harvest rice and Zari was the one to take the baby to Chamba for the operation. As soon as it became obvious that the family was poor, the hospital refused to operate. Discouraged, Zari returned home with Choti and the family became resigned to the baby's demise. One day a neighbour reported that he had seen a sign in the village advertising a free medical camp in Chamba. Dilip was annoyed with the neighbour for the suggestion, as he felt it raised false hopes for them. Zari was not to be discouraged, however, and went into the village to see for herself. Although she couldn't read, she asked someone else to read the sign for her. The interpreter told her that the medical camp was definitely free, and also that the doctors had many initials behind their names — so they had to be good, he said.

The rice harvest was almost complete, so that Chenu could join Zari for the journey to Chamba. Dilip was hard to convince, but finally agreed that Zari and Chenu could take the baby to Chamba the following Tuesday. He warned them not to get too hopeful. His experience was that people like themselves with no money didn't receive any breaks.

That evening Zari went to pray at the temple. She hadn't prayed for years, but after her prayer felt encouraged and told Chenu that she believed they would be accepted. Chenu was not as optimistic, and was even more skeptical when they arrived at the medical camp on Tuesday morning. The line-up was several hundred metres long. Chenu tried to tell her mother that they would never be accepted because the line-up was so long. But Zari refused to leave. At five, there was an announcement that the camp was unable to take any more applications for the day. The camp had expected to process one thousand patients a day, and had already taken over twelve hundred. Every department was overbooked, and the operating theatre was already booked solid for the week.

With that news, Zari and Chenu agreed that it was no use waiting and decided to go home. Just as they were ready to leave, a student from the ashram school approached them. He was distributing small pieces of paper, each with a number written on it. Zari and Chenu were handed the number 121. The student explained that in the morning, they would be number 121 to be interviewed. Zari stuffed the piece of paper in her bra, and told the student that they couldn't stay — they lived twenty kilometres away. The student suggested they sleep beside the river. Zari also told the student that they had not eaten all day and were hungry. He told them to go and settle in by the river near the bathing ghat and he would bring food. Zari remembered her trip to the temple and persuaded Chenu to try one more time.

Next morning when they arrived at the ashram at eight, several hundred people had already formed a queue. Both Chenu and Zari felt it was a waste of time to stand in line, but stayed anyway. By ten o'clock they were admitted to the room where the doctors were interviewing patients. Their hopes sank even further when a doctor told them that the operating theatre was booked solid for the week. Then he took out a pink piece of paper and wrote: "High priority: please schedule for today."

"I will operate," the doctor said as he handed the note to Chenu. "I also have a six-week-old daughter. We will operate on Choti today. Take this slip to the operating room desk." Both mother and grandmother thanked the doctor profusely. At the desk the attendant marked "2:00 p.m." on the slip, and handed it to Zari, explaining that they had just a cancellation for that time, and telling them to come back then. By now the manager of the ashram had realized that all these people waiting in the hot sun all day needed water to drink. He sent his assistant into town to buy plastic buckets and some students distributed water. He also told the kitchen staff to make enough food to feed an extra thousand people.

While Zari and Chenu had something to eat and drink, and Choti was fed from her mother's breast, they stayed in sight of the operating theatre. They were afraid they might lose out if their turn came and they were not there. At two o'clock, Zari took Choti to the O.T. desk. Chenu didn't want to be the one to hand over the baby — she was very shy and also she was afraid she might never see Choti again. Chenu had been warned that the operation was risky at such a young age. During the operation, while I waited with Zari, Chenu hovered around the O.T. After the surgery, mother and grandmother slept on the floor next to Choti's crib and for the last three days of Choti's recovery, Dilip also stayed. I managed a short good-bye to Choti and her family before being overcome with emotion.

At the end of five days, most of the medical group left to go back to New Delhi. A senior doctor, a nurse and myself stayed behind to attend to the post-operation patients. The doctor and I left four days later, leaving the nurse behind to attend to the last ten patients. The guru arranged for us to have lunch at a doctor's house in Dalhousie, and we had dinner at the same house where we had breakfast on the way to Chamba. At Pathankot we boarded an overnight train to New Delhi, then I switched to an early morning train to Calcutta. A few months later, Dr. Chamba sent me a Christmas card in which he wrote that one of the doctors had gone back to Chamba to do a follow-up one month after the medical camp and had reported that all of the operations had been successful.

Choti was not the only miracle in Chamba. There were at least four thousand miracles, as over four thousand patients passed through the medical camp. Many more were affected in one way or other, as many of these patients were accompanied by at least two family members who helped care for them. Eighty-seven operations were performed, not counting two hundred eye operations, and three hundred tooth extractions. The operations were successfully done without blood standing by. (According to my friends in the Canadian medical industry, this was a miracle.) The patients were willing to stand patiently in the blazing sun for hours. The ashram was willing to disrupt classes to provide food and water for thousands of extra people. The patients were treated by fourteen doctors who paid out of their own pockets for the privilege of caring for other human beings. I knew that I had truly been in the presence of miracles and miracle-workers.

.

Section 3

~

Mother Teresa
and the
Missionaries of Charity

Chapter 12

∽

The Missionaries
of Charity

Certainly the doctors and volunteers who provided free medical care were not the only miracle-workers I found in India. I also discovered the Missionaries of Charity, an international organization which has had significant impact on millions of lives around the globe. Even today, not many people recognize the name Missionaries of Charity, yet almost anyone recognizes the name of Mother Teresa, the founder.

In the early 1940s, Mother Teresa was the principal of a large Roman Catholic school, the Loreto School at Entally in Calcutta. She was good at her work and the school thrived. On occasion she travelled beyond the walls of the school compound and was always distressed by the sight of the starving people. Deeply troubled by what she saw, she felt something should be done to alleviate the people's suffering.

One day, enroute to her annual retreat, she was riding in the small gauge train (sometimes called the toy train) on her way to Darjeeling in the Himalayan foothills. On that train, God spoke to her and said, "You are to quit your job and go and work with the poorest of the poor in Calcutta." At last she had the clarity she had been seeking.

She went to her confessor, Father van Exem, and told him about her experience. He was enthusiastic about her decision and advised her to go and see the Archbishop. The Archbishop denied her request to quit her job and work with the poor. Eventually, through constant effort and strenuous negotiations by Father van Exem, permission was obtained. Mother Teresa received no financial support, however, and resolved to go begging if necessary. Although times were extremely difficult at first, Mother Teresa never wavered in her call. Miraculously, although lack of money was critical from time to time, it was always there when it was needed, and Mother Teresa never had difficulty in attracting new recruits.

After some time, she petitioned Rome to allow her to start a new order called the Missionaries of Charity. The organization was established in 1948. In 1997, just a few months before her death, Mother Teresa retired as the head of the organization. At that time, the Missionaries of Charity had almost six hundred homes all over the globe, and reputedly received approximately U.S. $50 million a year in donations in addition to container-loads of used clothing, and gifts of land and buildings. Their assets included numerous vehicles such as farm trucks and tractors, and several hundred ambulances. In Calcutta they also had a shop set up to build their own ambulances.

In human resources, the Missionaries of Charity in 1997 had over four thousand sisters, several thousand paid employees, and thousands of volunteers (mostly from the West). Many patients as well performed various volunteer functions. A separate branch called MC brothers worked in railway stations, did heavy physical work, or operated exclusively male institutions. Another affiliated international organization called Co-workers included hundreds of thousands of members located in the more affluent nations. One of the major functions of the Co-workers was to support the Missionaries of Charity work by collecting and shipping goods such as used clothes.

The charismatic style of Mother Teresa and her simple approach to the cause appealed greatly to her supporters. Record-keeping and waste were kept to an absolute minimum. There were no fax machines. Even telephones were not allowed for a long time. From Mother Teresa and all through the organization, an unselfish commitment remained steadfast, and that was to serve with love.

Chapter 13

~

Mother Teresa

Recently someone said to me: "You sure use 'Thank God' a lot!" I checked for a few days. Sure enough, the person was right. I knew where my habit came from. "Thank God, thank God, thank God." I heard that phrase frequently from Mother Teresa.

Much has been written about Mother Teresa, including a story about the time she was taken by a Catholic priest to observe a conflict at a border where both sides were engaged in firing at one another. She saw a group of children almost in the line of fire. Without hesitation, she stepped from behind her shelter and calmly walked over to the other side to rescue the children. Both sides stopped firing while she completed her mission. It was just one example of where her own welfare was not important, but God's children were.

Another story I heard about her came about at a convention in New Delhi. The club consisted of five hundred business presidents under the age of forty, and their spouses. The guest speakers were all high-profile people, including the president and prime minister of

India, and the industrial leaders from all over the world. Mother Teresa was also one of the guest speakers.

When Mother Teresa was handed a cheque for a million dollars for her work, she said that wasn't good enough. She wanted their time as well, she said, to volunteer in her AIDS home in New York. When she finished speaking, most of the powerful people were in tears. At the end of the session, the conventioneers were asked to complete an evaluation form and score the speakers on a scale of one to ten. The prime minister of India, who had delivered a powerful message, received mostly sixes and sevens. Mother Teresa was given straight tens — not because she was a good speaker, but because her message was simple and clear and unpretentious.

~

The first time I met Mother Teresa was in 1992. I suspected she would probably be too busy to meet me, but decided to go to her house. It was difficult to find. Just as I was about to abandon my search, I asked for directions. It turned out that I had walked past the house three times. I walked about fifty feet down an alley between two buildings. On the right, next to a double door, I saw a sign one inch by ten inches. The sign said simply: Mother Teresa. Next to the sign was a slot with the words "In" or "Out." "Out" was covered, thus indicating that Mother Teresa was in. A string dangled next to the sign and disappeared through a hole in the door. I thought the string might be a bell, and pulled it. Sure enough, I heard a bell ring inside the house. The door was opened instantly by a sister who said, "Come in," then went back to her conversation with another sister. I was quite taken aback by the informality of the place.

Inside, a group of volunteers stood in a circle chatting with each other. In the courtyard, several other sisters were busy washing saris in aluminum pails. I asked one of them where the church was and she said, "Up the stairs on the right." At the top of the stairs were rows of shoes, and I added my pair to them. Outside the chapel was a blackboard on which was written this statement: "If you want peace reach out to the poor." It was signed, "Mother Teresa MC." I stood there reflecting on the message. Of course I want peace, I thought, but what does it mean to reach out to the poor? Does she want money so she can reach out to the poor?

While I was deliberating, a sister rushed up to say that she would be right with me, she had to attend to something. She dashed through the door, but a few moments later reappeared and said: "Sorry to keep you waiting. How can I help you?" I could hardly believe what I was seeing. This wasn't an ordinary sister — this was Mother Teresa. I noticed how piercing her eyes were as they looked right at me. I saw a serene and wrinkled face peeking out from a frayed but clean sari. She was small in stature, less than five feet tall, with a stoop that betrayed her age and her arduous life. Her hands and feet were gnarled and twisted.

"Where are you from?" she asked, smiling slightly.

"Vancouver," I replied.

"Oh yes," she said, "we have sisters there. Will you pray for us?"

"Yes, Mother," I mumbled. I was awe-struck. I knew that she had been born in Albania, and had been a sister for almost seventy years. She looked and acted like a peasant, yet received respect from most of the world leaders, as well as royalty. And there she was right beside me. She took my right hand and, starting with the thumb, touched each of my fingers with her gnarled hand. As she touched each finger, she said very slowly, "You . . . Do . . . This . . . For . . . Me. Remember this when you are working with our patients." With the "Me," she was referring to God, not herself, she said. She repeated the phrase to me several more times, and later I often reflected on it while working.

"Do you have any family?" she asked.

"Yes," I said. She reached into a small box on the railing, took out several small medallions, touched them to her lips, and gave them to me.

"Are you staying for adoration?" she asked.

"Yes, Mother," I said.

"Good," she said, and that was the end of my first conversation with Mother Teresa.

She turned to an Indian couple waiting to see her. They both kissed her feet. They wanted to just take away a baby boy. Mother Teresa explained that they would have to apply and go through a whole adoption process, that there was no short cut. As the discussion went on, I admired Mother's patience. I was getting annoyed by the couple who were doggedly persisting. When the bell rang for adoration (church), I went inside the chapel. It was a large but plain room with grass mats spread out on the floor. A few stools and two benches were the only furniture except for a table serving as an altar. The congregation sat on the mats. I decided that I would be more comfortable on a bench. About ten minutes into the service, Mother Teresa quietly entered the chapel, knelt down and said a prayer, then leaned against the wall. I kept glancing at her and noticed that she frequently nodded off to sleep.

~

Over the years I had many chats with Mother Teresa. One time, she shared a dream she'd had and we laughed about it. She had died, and when she reached the Pearly Gates, she was asked by Saint Peter: "What are you doing here? There are no slums here, you better go back down!"

Whenever someone visited Mother House, Mother Teresa was always available for a brief talk. Her purpose was simple and twofold: to love God and to love the poor. Anything that differed from these two goals had little or no appeal to her. Even though she had received an abundance of recognition from all over the world, including a Nobel Prize, none of it had any effect on her principles as far as I could see. She stayed focused on the work. It was obvious that she didn't like the fuss that surrounded her. She often said, "It is all for God. I am nothing."

Once someone asked her a question about "the poor people in Calcutta." Mother Teresa's retort was: "The real poor are in America and Western Europe where they don't starve of malnutrition, but from a worse disease, that of loneliness." Having lived in both places, I agreed.

When Mother Teresa needed to fly somewhere, she just showed up at the airport. Every airline in the world flew her for no charge. Most insisted on putting her in first class, although her own choice was the economy section. Rather than see anything go to waste after the flight, she gathered all the leftover food in a bag and took it home for the poor. She never, never stopped thinking about the poorest of the poor. Another story went like this. The American branch of the Knights of Columbus (a Catholic men's group) gave her $5 million dollars and told her she would receive that same amount each year. She begged them not to do that, for then she would come dependent on it, and the security would spoil her style, which was to rely solely on God to provide. Knowing that the money was forthcoming she felt might take away her belief that God always provides, in His way and at His time. To her, that was more important than knowing the money was coming.

~

Mother Teresa was pictured many times sitting on a sidewalk with a man's head in her lap. She would be giving him a drink of water, and at the same time taking care of his emotional and spiritual needs and thanking God for the opportunity to serve him. Working with her and her volunteers brought a renewed purpose to my life. Whenever I hear myself saying I can't, I try to remember Mother Teresa's conviction that all things are possible with God.

Not everyone is a believer in Mother Teresa. For example, British author Christopher Hitchens did a BBC television documentary called "Hell's Angels" and subsequently wrote a book called *The Missionary Position: Mother Teresa In Theory and Practice* (London: Verso, 1995). I personally don't feel I need to defend Mother Teresa. She was quite capable of defending herself. It is true that anyone in the public spotlight lives under a microscope. Although she may have made mistakes, I am sure that it was never with malicious intent. Personally I disagreed with some of her beliefs — on birth control, for example. That did not prevent me from working with her and supporting her (or God's) goals. She never varied from her purpose, which was loving, caring and sharing.

After she died in 1997, this clay figure of Mother Teresa was placed where she had so often sat in the chapel. Everyone who sees it agrees that it is startlingly lifelike.

Chapter 14

❧

Sisters

I am always amazed at how I can be so sure of something one day and then need to change my mind a few days later. One example is the way I first thought of the Missionaries of Charity sisters. Before I even met the sisters, I decided that they were "old maids" — dedicated, but without feelings, frustrated, boring, sombre — the list went on. They became that for me as soon as I chose to judge and allowed my anti-Catholic position influence me. When I actually met some of the sisters, I took some negative incidents and expanded them, and decided they were poor clones of Mother Teresa. Over the years, I realized how wrong I was.

In today's world, the number of people attending church or joining religious orders seems to be declining. It is very rare, however, for sisters to resign from the Missionaries of Charity order. They take a vow of poverty and live dormitory-style. Each sister has three saris: one to wear, one for the wash, and one for an emergency. A crucifix, a rosary, and perhaps a sweater are the only other possessions. Most of the sisters are of Indian descent, even in foreign countries, and the work they do is varied. I personally know of two sisters with medical degrees. Some are trained as nurses, others as teachers, and many do medically related jobs. All associated with the Missionaries of Charity are expected to serve cheerfully. Their speciality is taking care of those no one else is willing to care for.

∽

The last time I was in India, in the fall of 1997, the sisters at Shanti Nagar (the community for people suffering from leprosy) were already getting excited about a wedding eight months away. The groom would be one of the boys they had raised since he was three years old. A number of the sisters invited me to attend the wedding, and assured me that it would be beautiful. They were so proud that he had turned out well, and was happy, and they wanted to share their joy. Many of the children raised by the sisters at Shanti Nagar had married. Each young woman got to wear a wedding dress — in fact, they all wore the same one, which the sisters altered innumerable times to fit. I was told the dress was probably twenty years old. No biological mother could have been more excited than the sisters became on these occasions. The biological mother may have had concerns about the wedding happening without flaws, but the sisters didn't fret about such details. They trusted that the outcome would be God's will and they would abide by His decision.

One day, as I strolled along Pope Paul Boulevard in Shanti Nagar, an excited sister approached me and said, "Have you seen our one-day-old baby?" I went along to see. When we got to the nursery, a group of about twenty sisters and girls were crowding around the baby and waiting for their turn to hold her. When I saw the baby, my initial reaction was shock. All I saw was a nose, no eyes, and where the mouth should be, a hole. My shock lasted but a few seconds — by this time I had learned from Mother Teresa to find beauty in even the most deformed persons. What made it easier was all the fuss the sisters were making over their new charge. The excitement was contagious, and very quickly I too was excited about having such a small addition added to our nursery. Since I was a regular visitor to the nursery, I looked forward to playing with the new baby as well as with the other children.

Two days later, while I was away with the boys, the baby died, and was buried that same afternoon. Most of us had mixed emotions. We had all loved her, and yet we knew she would have had a difficult existence. We dealt with our loss by sharing our thoughts and supporting each other and resolving that we had work to do and life had to go on. Together, we thanked God for the joy she had brought us. Once again I found myself very moved by the sisters, who cared so much, and loved so deeply, and derived so much strength from their faith.

On another day, the sister in charge of the boys' home asked whether I would like to go to a concert where the boys would be performing. I had finished my work for the day and said I would be delighted. About twenty of us jammed into an ambulance to travel the forty kilometres to the next town. We arrived at a huge complex of Catholic schools and were escorted to the VIP section. My companion, Father Jake, and I escaped from this section to sit in the back. When our truancy was discovered, we were brought back into the VIP section to sit on the plush couches. We were introduced to the dignitaries and served tea and cookies.

Sitting next to me was Sister S., who informed me that I was to sing in front of the audience. She knew that Sister Superior and I had practised the songs, "How Great Thou Art" and "Amazing Grace." I agreed that I would sing "How Great Thou Art" when called. Just to make sure I wouldn't escape again, Sister S. stayed in the seat right next to me and interpreted the Hindi performances for me. When the various schools began to compete against each other in a Bible quiz, Sister S. and I decided to compete against each other. Out of a possible 30, the score was Michael: 1; Sister S.: 28 (neither of us knew the answer to one of the questions). We chuckled together, teased each other, and became good friends from that day on.

The performance by "our" boys was outstanding. Most of us had to fight back tears. All by themselves, the boys had learned and practised the songs, borrowed a set of three drums, and had dressed in dark slacks and white T-shirts. The T-shirts as well as everything else they wore was donated to the Missionaries of Charity. I wish the donors could have been there — the Saint Louis baseball camp, a restaurant in Chicago and the Northern California Hikers Club would have been proud. The boys' singing was very upbeat. Judging from the applause, they were a shoo-in for first prize. Unfortunately, they finished second.

The concert dragged on and on. The audience was getting restless. When the organizers finally asked me if I was ready to sing, I declined. The organizers agreed that it was time to bring the event to a halt since half of the audience had already left.

After the concert, we stood by the road for an hour waiting for our ambulance. We took this opportunity to congratulate the boys on a job well done. They enjoyed all the accolades. When the ambulance arrived, we began a boisterous sing-along. When one of the sisters asked me to sing for them, I agreed, and started with "Kumbaya, my lord . . ." Just then, we heard a loud bang. Our tire had exploded! Everyone teased me about blowing up the tire with my awful singing.

The reason the ambulance had been late to pick us up in the first place was that it had had an flat tire. Now we were stranded beside the road without a spare. We spent two hours sitting beside the road in the dark while the driver took the tire away to get it repaired. During that time, some of the boys snuggled up to the sisters and had a nap. One of the sisters lay on the seat with her head in the lap of one of the boys. I was deeply touched by how the sisters and the boys were relating and how much they cared for another. Once we were on our way again, we had yet another flat tire. Since we were by that time just over a kilometre from home, we all disembarked and walked home singing and dancing in the dark, quiet countryside. I realized what a fabulous day I had had with the sisters and the boys —a time full of fun and laughter. I wouldn't have believed it a few years earlier!

Another discovery I made about the sisters was that even though they took vows to give their lives to Jesus, they continued to be interested and involved in their former lives. Like the rest of us, they had concerns about parents, siblings, nieces, and nephews. One told me the story of how she had asked for and received a transfer from Africa back to India in order to be near her ailing mother. Another sister was the guardian of her teenage niece and nephew. I knew the niece and nephew very well. The niece lived with the sisters in another convent where she was taking a computer course. The nephew lived in the same facility as his aunt. The sister had the same problems as any other parent. When her young charges asked for money or for permission to go to a show or concert, she had the same difficult decisions to make, and asked the same questions: Who are you going with? How are you getting there? How are you getting home? She also had the same worries: Are they going to drink? Smoke? Get into any other mischief? I watched the three of them interact and my impression was that they could be a model of an ideal family.

When I became open to the sisters as human beings as well as dedicated sisters, I had wonderful conversations with some. Inevitably, we had many religious discussions. In addition, I was always interested in asking them such questions as: What if you were transferred to a far-away place? What if you were demoted? What if you cannot get along with another sister? I had seen a clash of personalities between sisters, but didn't know how they were resolved. The sisters I talked with told me that when issues came up, they would pray for a solution and get their own egos out of the way. Being aware that the ego was the problem and believing that their purpose was much more important than their individual concerns seemed to resolve most of their issues.

One thing most of the sisters had in common was surrender and acceptance. I knew sisters who had been in the position of superior, then been transferred to another location to become an ordinary sister. In fact, it was common practice to demote a superior for a while and then to promote her back to the original position. As far as I could tell, this practice seemed to build trust rather than anger or resentment. It did not seem to present a major problem for most sisters, although a few shared with me that sometimes when they were demoted they wondered whether it was a reflection on their abilities. Their solution was to take the problem into their prayer life and resolve the difficulty.

The Missionaries of Charity sisters of course had a great teacher in Mother Teresa. Initially I predicted that her retirement and death would have a severe impact on the future of the whole organization. I now conclude that the impact will hardly be noticeable. The new superior general, Sister Nirmala, is highly respected and has inherited a philosophy and a constitution that should withstand any pressure. The over four thousand sisters have been well trained, and have the same purpose and goals as Mother Teresa — to satisfy the thirst of Christ by serving the poorest of the poor. In their homespun and simple white-and-blue saris, they continue to shine their light into the world's darkest places.

Sister Nirmala and Mother Teresa, 1997

Chapter 15

~

Volunteers

On my first trip to India in 1992, one of the stops was Kalighat, a home run by Mother Teresa and her army of sisters and volunteers. Our guide was Tony, a volunteer from San Francisco, California. Tony ushered us through the home, explained the work, and described his experiences of living in Calcutta and volunteering. I'd seen and heard enough to know that this was what I wanted to try. The next year I went back and, like so many other volunteers, I have returned year after year.

My first day as a volunteer, as I sat waiting to begin work, I asked myself: What am I doing here? Look at these poor people. I don't think I can handle this. I think I'll run. I let myself feel all these emotions, then decided to stay. It was a decision I have never regretted. My wage for donating my time in India has been transformation. The rewards have been the opening of my heart and a new lifestyle based on peace and serenity.

~

Each of Mother Teresa's houses in Calcutta had a different purpose. Some houses cared for medical patients or children while others cared for those with leprosy, AIDS, or emotional handicaps. In Kalighat, where I worked, the primary purpose was to care for the dying and the destitute. Patients in need of medical treatment were taken to a local hospital. There were limited medical facilities in Kalighat; many of the patients were beyond medical help and came to die in dignity with many people to care for them. Many did die, and their bodies were disposed of in accordance with their religious custom.

Kalighat, 1996

Andy, the man in charge of volunteers, gave me my first job. I was to feed a man breakfast, which consisted of puffed rice with sliced bananas. I loaded the spoon with puffed rice and pointed it towards the man's mouth. When he opened his mouth, I saw that all he had was two brown front teeth. I thought: How ugly, I think I may get sick. Several minutes later, Andy came by and in an angry voice said, "For goodness sake, pick him up and hold him! How would you like to lie in bed eating?" I didn't relish the thought of picking the man up, but I did it anyway. The patient responded with a broad toothless smile, and resumed his extremely slow eating. I was annoyed and impatient and wishing I were elsewhere, but stuck with the task. Gradually, my resentment turned into compassion as I noticed how the man loved being held. Then more thoughts niggled at me. I was concerned about what the other volunteers might think. There I was, holding a person of the same sex. Finally, I looked around and was relieved to see others doing the same thing.

My second assignment was to assist another volunteer with picking maggots from the flesh wound of a patient. The other volunteer worked the tweezers to pick out the maggots while I held a bottle of ether with a squirt top. Just the heads of the maggots were sticking out of the wound. I would spray them with ether, which caused them to crawl to the surface, and my partner would snatch them. I also held a dish in which to put the maggots. When we were finished, I dropped the contents of my dish in the toilet and vomited.

After work that day, I was exhausted as well as elated. I realized that I was elated not only because I had got through the day's tasks but also because I felt noble. I knew that this kind of thinking could and probably would get me into a lot of difficulty. I had been sober for two years, and in my program of recovery I had gained some insight into the dangers of false pride and an exploding ego. I knew the antidote was genuine humility. Looking back on my feelings that morning, I concluded that I hadn't come to help the patients, but to help myself, and to learn from the lessons that I was experiencing. In other words, I hadn't come to help the patients — how could I? — but to serve them.

While I was reflecting on my first day, I was also wondering how to get back to my hotel. I had taken a taxi to work. A group of volunteers passed by me, and one young woman said, "You look lost." I said I was just debating on how to get home, and she asked me where I was staying. It turned out we were all going the same place, and she asked me to join them. We rode back on the Metro (underground subway). I was indeed amazed that this group of people at least twenty years younger than I was accepted me as a peer. The chatter on the way home was about the work, or about where we were from. Everyone but me was from one of the European countries.

When we reached Sudder Street where we all lived, we crammed into the already overcrowded Blue Sky Café. The seating in this restaurant was on picnic tables and benches. To me, the energy in the room was extremely positive. Most of the customers were doing volunteer work for various organizations in Calcutta. Ralph from the United States went around the restaurant organizing a baseball game for the afternoon. About twenty people showed up. For a bat we used a two-by-four board and for a ball we used a tennis ball. The game was fun even with that equipment.

It was easy to organize activities either by going to the local restaurants or by spreading the word at work. The Mother House, our headquarters, was also a good place to promote events since most volunteers visited there regularly for Mass, or meetings, or just to say hello to Mother Teresa. Events included movies, meetings, travel to other hospices, picnics, plays, concerts, and sports. Everyone was accepted. I never felt out of place, even though I was usually much older than the rest of the volunteers. Although the volunteers I met while working for Mother Teresa were of all ages and from all over the world, most were from Europe and in their twenties. Many stayed for a week or so, while a few stayed for years. For example, Bernie from Ireland worked on her own (that is, not with any organization). Her territory was the Shealda Railway Station where she made daily rounds to care for people who called that station home.

At times the job had special rewards. One long-term patient hadn't walked for years. Day after day, one volunteer massaged the patient's legs, until one day the patient took his first step in front of a gathering of volunteers. The patient received a round of applause and many hugs. A few volunteers even shed tears of joy.

Another day, a patient asked me to pull a tooth. I asked several sisters what to do. They informed me that tooth-pulling was beyond our scope. I went back to the patient to inform him of the decision, but he wouldn't accept that answer. I went to Andy and he agreed to help. He said, "I will pray and you pull!" Both of us were tense. When he started to pray, I pulled hard. The tooth was so loose that it came out easily. We both had a good laugh. All that tension and praying when the tooth was about to fall out on its own! This was just one of many funny and emotional events.

One activity I chose many times was to go a home in Howrah, across the river from Calcutta. The home was operated by the Missionaries of Charity (MC) brothers. On Sunday mornings, about two hundred young street boys would show up. In one corner of the courtyard, there were twelve water taps where we would scrub the layers of dirt off the boys and encourage them to wash their clothes.

Other volunteers would mend the clothes, put dressings on wounds, cut hair, or play games. Then the boys ate a meal and went back to the streets. Many lived in the massive Howrah Railway Station complex nearby. Afterwards, soaked to the skin with water, we volunteers were given a meal by the Brothers.

For the first several years I worked with the Missionaries of Charity, I managed to avoid dealing with those who had died. Inevitably, someone asked me to help clean up a body, wrap it in a shroud and deliver it to the burning place. The following year, I was working as an undertaker in Calcutta. For three and a half months, I was in charge of disposing of about two hundred and fifty bodies. Most were Hindus, and those I would take to the nearby burning ghats. The Muslims were sent to a Muslin burial ground and the Christians were put in a plain box casket and buried. With the Christians, I was there for the entire process. I assisted with lowering the casket and remained at the graveside until the body was covered.

The experience of being an undertaker was very positive for me and I wanted to share that experience with others. For that reason, I always selected new volunteers to assist me. Some weren't ready for the challenge. They couldn't get used to handling dead people or didn't know how to deal with the feelings that death raised for them. Most, however, found it to be a very moving and positive involvement. I received some criticism for employing uninitiated volunteers to help me, but believed it was worth the risk. We always handled the bodies respectfully, and sent them on their way with love and dignity.

~

On Thursdays, all the Missionaries of Charity volunteers were required to take a day off. On quite a few occasions, I took a forty-five-minute train ride to visit a nearby leprosy settlement located at Titagarh. This settlement interested me because there was a wide range of opportunities for volunteering. There were facilities for surgery, and since Titagarh tried to produce much of its own food, there was also much work to be done in the gardens. One sight that never failed to impress me was a very long, narrow building where hand looms were set up. These looms and their operators produced all the saris for the Missionaries of Charity sisters and most of the bed sheets for the thousands of beds within the huge organization. But the real attraction was the patients, whether they were working or bedridden. Their enthusiastic greetings and generous smiles lit up everyone around them.

On my days off or when I needed a change of pace, I sometimes went to a Calcutta district called Cosipore, where Dr. Jack Pleger had an outdoor clinic. The Missionaries of Charity was not usually well equipped to deal with medical needs, but Dr. Jack and his Calcutta Rescue organization certainly were. When the volunteers arrived at the compound at 8:30 a.m., already hundreds of patients were waiting, sitting on their haunches, to see one of the doctors. The volunteers began by setting up the pharmacy and counting out pills into small envelopes. New volunteers received a ten-minute training. Throughout the compound were miniature departments such as birth control, Vitamin A injections, dressings (to change dressings and give injections), and food.

The twelve doctors arrived about 9:00 a.m. After each doctor interviewed a patient, a volunteer took the patient's chart and prepared the prescriptions. Pills were put in an envelope made of used computer paper with the blank side out. Instead of written instructions, each envelope was rubber-stamped with symbols saying how and when to take the medicine. The volunteer then took the prescription to the patient and through the aid of an interpreter gave verbal instruction about how to use the medicine.

Although the compound was covered with a tarp, it became stifling hot. By the end of my shift, I was usually exhausted and had sore feet from being on them all day. Although the personal contact with the patients wasn't as intimate as at Mother Teresa's homes, I found the contributions of Dr. Jack and his volunteers miraculous too.

~

On one of my visits to the Missionaries of Charity, I was appointed one of the coordinators to guide volunteers and free the sisters for other work. At the end of each work day, I would wait at the front of the ward to debrief volunteers if necessary. Most of us had little or no experience in dealing with sickness and death. Often by the end of the shift we were emotionally wrung out. An arm around the shoulder, a hug, or a kind word often helped.

Sometimes nothing was enough to offset the kind of work we did. On one occasion, for instance, three young men arrived for their first day's work. They were eager to contribute and were a most welcome sight, since this day there was a severe shortage of volunteers. Not only were we short-staffed, but we also had more critically ill patients than usual. The young men said they were going to stay for three weeks, and assured me they were looking forward to a challenging time. It was the roughest day I had ever spent. With four deaths and many very sick patients, we had been run off our feet. At the end of the shift, the young men and I sat down and discussed the day. They said that they were "wiped" physically as well as emotionally and couldn't imagine doing another day. They never came back.

Many volunteers came to serve the poor, and were a delight to work with. Others came to change things or fix things. One young woman wanted to seek revenge for a couple of female patients who had been burned. She decided that they were victims of dowry burnings and was going to find the men who did it, and make them pay. Another volunteer searched the streets looking for new patients and dragged them in whether they wanted to come or not. Other volunteers decided to adopt a boy or a girl and or a whole family. These volunteers likely meant well, but soon discovered that changing and fixing were not consistent with the desires and goals of God as Mother Teresa saw them.

Sometimes volunteers insisted that the procedures used in their country were right, and the approach used in India, or the approach used by Mother Teresa, was wrong. One volunteer asked for a spoon for a patient. I went to a drawer to get him one. He wouldn't accept the spoon, saying, "I need fifty of them." When asked why, he said, "None of these people have spoons and they need them." When I suggested that everyone was comfortable eating with their hands, he got angry, untied his apron, and threw it on the floor in a rage. He mumbled something about Mother Teresa being mean and stormed out of the door. That was the last we saw of him.

A few volunteers came to Kalighat to save, rather than to serve, the dying. A group of American fundamentalist Christians came to work at Kalighat for just one day. At the end of the day, the group's leader came to me looking very distraught and told me how terrible it was about the man in bed thirty-six.

"You mean the one who died this morning?" I asked.

"That's right. How terrible," he repeated.

"Oh no," I replied, "it's not terrible. He was suffering very badly and now he has peace at last."

"Was he a Hindu?" he asked.

"Yes," I answered, "I took his body to the burning ghat."

"That is too bad," the man said. "I didn't save him, and now he is in Hell." I had to walk away, for I felt very angry. The patient had been brave and sweet even though he was in extreme pain. I had become quite fond of him, and admired his courage. I felt frustrated by this man who was so sure about someone else's fate. I had to admit to myself, however, that for many years I had a similar outlook. That kind of attitude was one of the reasons that I gradually left the Christian Reformed (Calvinist) church. With Mother Teresa's example, I now chose to believe that God loved everyone with no exception.

Mother Teresa's belief and practice was simply that love was the greatest medicine. Some people with medical backgrounds, such as doctors or nurses, had difficulty accepting that. Since I didn't have any medical training, I soon gave up trying to determine who was wrong or right medically. But after years of being in the middle of such controversy, I decided that it seemed much kinder to let a person who was beyond help medically have a peaceful death in an atmosphere of love, rather than undergo an operation that was not needed, or die alone in a hospital.

~

I have thought many times about the value of the volunteers in Mother Teresa's houses. Given the number of patients and the work required, it would be very difficult for the sisters and the paid staff to give the kind of care the patients received without the volunteers. From Mother Teresa's viewpoint, the opportunity to serve was a gift to the volunteers, as were any lessons that came out of the serving. I am very thankful to have had the chance to be with people as they died and to work with Mother Teresa, the sisters, and the other volunteers. In my experience working in her houses, the more I disagreed, or the more conflict I had, the greater my lessons were. My greatest lessons have been to swing towards less judgment, and to melt my hard heart.

Chapter 16

~

Shanti Nagar

Shanti Nagar, also known as Peace City. Population: six hundred leprosy patients, twelve sisters, one priest — and sometimes me. When Mother Teresa started this community in the state of West Bengal, she envisioned it as a place for leprosy sufferers to come for medical care and a place of comfort and peace where they would feel accepted and loved. It often happens that when people get this dreaded disease, their families and communities reject them, and they have nowhere to turn. Over the years many lepers have found peace and better health at Shanti Nagar.

~

Again and again, volunteers with whom I worked in Calcutta raved about their great experiences at Shanti Nagar. I too applied to do a stint as a volunteer and was accepted. I left Calcutta, boarded a train, and five hours later arrived at the Chittyranjan railway station. I braced myself for the usual onslaught of porters, beggars, vendors, and taxi drivers. Amazingly there weren't any.

This time, I was the only one disembarking from the train, and the handful of people lounging on the benches just ignored me. How different this was from the big cities, where upon arrival I always felt like jumping back on board the train to escape the overwhelming mass of humanity pushing, shoving, and shouting.

Feeling relieved, I slung my backpack over my shoulder and happily sauntered towards the town square looking for a taxi. None were to be seen. I walked over to a cluster of bicycle rickshaws and found that most of the operators were lolling in the back of their vehicles. Not one of them seemed interested in communicating with me to find out whether I needed transportation. I turned around and set off to find another way to get to my destination.

As I walked away, an approaching rickshaw driver asked, "Shanti Nagar?" I nodded with relief and negotiated a fare of 10 rupees. I climbed aboard the rickety rickshaw and the strong muscled legs of the driver pedalled towards the outskirts of the town. The country road was full of potholes, hilly and without traffic. It was scenic and peaceful. When we got to the first hill the driver got off and pushed the rickshaw uphill. I hopped off as well and joined him in pushing it. On the other side of the hill we climbed back on the rickshaw and coasted down. The downhill ride was hair-raising as with frightening speed we bounced in and out of potholes. I half expected the fragile rickshaw to collapse or fall apart, but we managed to get to the bottom without damage. Again I disembarked at the foot of the hill to make the push upwards lighter, left my bag in the rickshaw, and walked up the hill. Several minutes later the rickshaw driver caught up with me and I climbed back on. We repeated this procedure several more times until we reached Shanti Nagar.

Inside the gate was a paved road called Pope Paul Boulevard, a wide, well-kept lane lined with trees on both sides. It made a wonderful first impression. I was told that the sisters were resting and shouldn't be disturbed, and was invited to wait for them in the guest dining hall. There, I too took advantage of siesta time and fell asleep. After my rest I was introduced to Father Jake, an eighty-year-old Roman Catholic priest who was living out his retirement years at Shanti Nagar. Anna, another volunteer, joined us. While we were having tea, the sister in charge of volunteers came by. She hadn't been told of my visit and was not expecting me. The policy for volunteers was to have only men or only women there at any one time. With Anna there already, my presence was a problem. Fortunately, there was an empty room next to the main dormitory, and I could take up residence there. Anna was due to leave in three days anyway.

After tea, Father Jake gave me a guided tour of the walled-in community. He introduced me to all twelve cows by name, but said he didn't know the names of the chickens, ducks, and geese. Behind the barns stood a long narrow building which housed the outpatients' clinic where twice a week some patients and sisters dispensed drugs. Our next stop was the mango groves and banana fields. Afterwards, we chatted with some of the workers in the vegetable gardens. They discussed their continuing problem of thefts during the night. The previous night about a dozen cabbages had been stolen. They intended to organize a night shift and, with the help of dogs, were hoping to solve the theft problem.

Next to the gardens and at the end of the road were rice paddies, and a little further down was the graveyard. It was customary to bury the bodies on top of each other so each grave could hold three corpses. We continued our tour, passing by the kitchens and Boys Town, the schoolboys' residence. Then we stopped at Shishu Bhavan, the children's home, where babies, small children, and young girls lived. To the delight of the babies in their cribs, we tickled a few tummies as we passed through. We also went to see some of the hospital wards. As soon as we entered a ward, those who weren't bedridden jumped up and touched Father Jake's feet as well as mine. I asked Father how to respond to such adulation. He said, "Place your hands on their head and give them a blessing." It took me a while to adjust to this kind of homage, but as time went on it became more natural. We spent some time chatting with the patients. I was impressed by all I saw in this remarkable complex, and especially by the warmth of Father Jake.

That evening, Anna, Father Jake and I were joined at dinner by Roger, a young seminarian who was also a patient. We shared food and laughter in the brightly lit dining room of the guest house. After dinner, Roger left to play cricket with some of the boys from Boys Town. Anna, Father Jake and I lingered for several more hours talking about a variety of subjects. Religion was at the top of the list. Father also told some excellent jokes. Originally from Belgium, he had spent the last forty years in India, mostly in Calcutta. At one point, Anna asked if she could receive Communion the next day. As she was not a Roman Catholic, Father Jake refused her request. I felt quite sad about this exclusion, but for me it was the only low point of the evening. When I went to bed later that night, I felt warm and fulfilled and slept soundly.

The next morning, I attended my first Mass at Shanti Nagar. Roman Catholic Mass was celebrated twice a day at Shanti Nagar, and Sister Superior had broadly hinted that attendance was a condition of my stay. The service was in Hindi. In the past when I was forced to go to church, I would feel anger and frustration, especially when I heard words like: "We beg of you" and "Please forgive us our sins." To me, that made God sound like a monster. On this occasion, though, and for the rest of the two weeks, I used the time at Mass to sit, reflect and contemplate. I relished the time of private peaceful reflection and enjoyed singing the hymns.

Father Jake had invited two men from the congregation to join us for breakfast. Gurdeep, a sturdy muscular man in his mid-twenties, was a student at the police academy nearby. He was a jovial addition to our morning meal. Hiran, a religious zealot about forty, kept trying to convert me to Catholicism. He tried to persuade Father Jake to assist him, but Father Jake cleverly avoided becoming involved in Hiran's scheme. Both Hiran and Gurdeep offered to show me around the area. Hiran worked at the locomotive factory and hoped to arrange a tour for me the following Tuesday. (Unfortunately, he did not receive permission for me to tour the factory.) Gurdeep didn't have classes on Sundays, and had the afternoon free to show me around. We agreed to go after lunch.

Father Jake mentioned that he had to officiate at a funeral that morning. One of the patients we had talked with the previous night had died. I wanted to be at the funeral because I was fascinated with the local custom of burying three bodies in one grave. After breakfast, I walked to the graveyard. The sister who was supervising the digging of the grave explained that since it was Sunday, the regular staff had a day off. She had recruited some patients to dig the grave and was supervising to make sure it was done right. Everyone was in high spirits — those who worked as well as bystanders. Sister had cut a stick and kept measuring the hole as the diggers kept digging. Frequently I peered into the hole to see whether I could detect the remains of the previous body. Although the hole was dug very deep, nothing turned up and it became clear that this was the first body to be buried there. When the sister was satisfied with the size of the excavation, she sent for the body. We did not have to wait for Father Jake. Since the deceased was a Hindu and not a Christian, the priest had decided to keep a previous engagement and go on a picnic with the bishop.

Fifty patients gathered around the grave while the body was brought out on the bed in which the patient had died and placed next to the freshly dug cavity. Two of the grave-diggers jumped into the hole and two patients lowered the shroud-covered body. While this was going on, the sister read out loud from a book and two male patients on the opposite side of the grave gave a response to every sentence. The response was "Sancta Maria." Both men had a deep voice. They stood with their arms locked together — actually stumps locked together, as both had lost their arms to leprosy. One was blind as well. I fought back tears. The ceremony was simple yet beautiful in its reverence.

In the middle of the ceremony, however, people who stood closest to the grave began to snicker as they peered into the hole. The sister who was reading stopped to investigate and I joined her to have a look. It couldn't be more clear that the body didn't fit; the hole was too short or the corpse too tall. Who knew which? Amusement prevailed over solemnity, even with the sister. Now what? A conference was called. It was decided to enlarge the hole. The body was pulled into a corner, feet up in the air, while the men below proceeded to dig a recess at the bottom to fit the head in. When the head was firmly in place, the ceremony continued. After that, the grave was closed with soil. Flowers were handed to all the participants and placed on the grave, also smoking sticks of incense. It was a beautiful conclusion to a remarkably moving incident.

After lunch, Gurdeep, the chap from the police academy, made arrangements with some of the boys from Boys Town to prepare three bicycles. Anna had asked to join us. All three of us were adept at riding bicycles, and with Gurdeep leading the way, we headed for a sandy road. We pedalled through three tiny settlements and were always greeted with broad smiles and friendly shouts of "Namaste" (roughly translated as: "When I am in mine and you are in yours, there is only one of us"). Each time we stopped in one of the villages we attracted a crowd of curious onlookers. Life in rural India seemed tranquil: women carrying huge loads of water, coal or firewood on their heads, children playing simple games with bits of wood, baby goats getting into mischief, and dogs lying in the sun. Nobody was in a hurry; people appeared to accept life as it came to them.

We met a few other cyclists, and quite a few pedestrians. We cycled past sand dunes, a target practice range, the police academy, and the lake on which the academy was situated. The sun was hot, but not bothersome as we were having a superb time. Eight kilometres later we came to a enormous hydro-electric dam. On top of the dam was a variety of tea shops. We looked around until we found one that offered shelter against the heat, and ordered cold drinks and Indian sweets. It was refreshing to sit down for a rest and talk. Between Anna and Gurdeep a tremendous bonding was taking place. He called her "Mom." She was in her fifties and he in his twenties. If it weren't for the fact that their features were totally different, it might have worked! Next to the tea shops were boat rental outlets. Anna was keen on hiring one, but Gurdeep and I balked at the asking price. Anna persevered, and reluctantly we agreed to pay what seemed like a king's ransom. I stretched out and basked in the sun and rested up for the return bike ride, all the while humming: "Cruising down the river on a Sunday afternoon . . ."

After the boat ride, Gurdeep gave us a tour of the police academy and took us to luxury cabins situated on a cliff overlooking the lake. The cabins were for the use of visiting officials, but since there were no visiting officials at that time, we were free to enjoy the surroundings. A friend of Gurdeep served us refreshments — it was VIP treatment. We enjoyed lounging around until it was time to return to Shanti Nagar. At supper we shared our experiences with Father Jake. He said that he was sorry to have missed the outing since he enjoyed riding a bicycle.

For the next two weeks, Father Jake and I went bike riding everyday. Later I found out that Sister Superior did not approve of him going by himself because of his advanced age. I soon learned that he enjoyed these outings so much that he would overdo it, and became exhausted. Every once in a while he would fall off his bike and acquire major bruises. I never told Sister Superior, as he was such a dear man.

When I had been a guest for two days, I still hadn't done any work. I kept asking for work, but wasn't assigned any, and was beginning to feel frustrated. I felt I needed to work to earn my keep. While I was walking around, I saw two men digging a foundation for a new building. They had three shovels, so I grabbed one of them and started to dig. They protested, but since they didn't talk English, I didn't know why and kept digging. People who came by were amused and snickered as they talked with my fellow workers. I couldn't figure out what I was doing wrong. Finally, someone sent for Father Jake, who came over and explained that this type of work was only for people of low caste and certainly not for a white person. When I told him that I was enjoying the work and wanted to continue, he applauded my choice and said that it was an excellent lesson for the Indian way of thinking. Most of the sisters, however, didn't endorse my work and were uncomfortable with it.

At lunch, Father Jake said that it was everyone's custom to rest after lunch. After the rest, tea would be served. I went into my room to read, but fell asleep. My morning's work had been strenuous. Having a nap after lunch became a pleasant pastime every day. At tea I was asked whether I would like to shave patients the next day. I said yes, I was very good at it, having done lots of shaving in Calcutta. When I was shown the tools, however, there was only a straight razor which I didn't know how to use.

After tea, Father and I headed off for what was to become our daily bike ride. He was very much liked in the community, and was always greeted warmly wherever we went. First we went to the next village so that I could buy a safety razor. It gave a purpose to our bike ride. We didn't find a razor there, but later when we stopped at the tea shop across the street of our own village, I saw a display of safety razors and bought one, as well as a supply of blades. Father Jake felt embarrassed that we had gone all that distance to find razor blades when they were available this close. I assured him I had enjoyed the trip to the village.

The following morning, one of the workers handed me a white coat to wear for my role as barber. The first ward I went to had twelve beds. I walked down the aisle looking for my first customer. To my surprise, there were no takers. The patients were talking amongst themselves. After ten rejections, I asked the only English-speaking patient what they were talking about. He said they thought it strange that this white guy would want to give them a shave, and did I know how to do it? I told him I was well qualified and asked him to tell that to the others. Finally, the fellow in the last bed took a chance and allowed me to give him a shave. Those that could get out of bed crowded around to watch. They must have been impressed, for ten out of the twelve asked for a shave and two asked to have their hair cut. Word spread around the other wards and soon I was putting in a solid morning doing shaves and haircuts. I drew no blood and had only one complaint that the haircut was too slow. Every morning after that, I set up shop in the courtyard unless the sisters requested that I go to a ward.

After five days, an English-speaking patient asked if I could cut fingernails. Boasting, I said that I was an expert in that area as well. After I had clipped his nails, another patient also wanted a manicure. When I'd cut the fingernails of that patient, someone asked me if I did toenails as well. A large audience gathered around, with everyone talking Hindi amongst themselves. My patient extended his foot towards my hand. I had been told that leprosy was spread by body fluids and this man's foot was weeping. I hesitated. The audience was watching me and I realized that I was on trial. I had won their confidence and stood to lose it in this moment of confrontation. I said to myself: You have survived so far, go for it. And I cut his toenails.

Some patients at Shanti Nagar, 1996

On Thursday morning, we had our biweekly visit by a surgeon. Father Jake and the surgeon persuaded me to join the operating team. They explained that people with leprosy lost sensitivity in their limbs and often injured themselves badly. Some burned themselves on hot stoves because they didn't feel the heat in time to avoid serious injury. Others walking barefoot cut their feet on glass or stones and did not realize that they were hurt until the wound became gangrenous. After breakfast, I followed the surgeon to the operating room. In the courtyard, twenty-two patients waited. The surgeon went to each of the patients and quickly examined them. A sister followed with a note-pad and kept track of what the surgeon prescribed as treatment. We then went into the operating theatre where I was given a gown, mask and gloves. I was very nervous and asked Father Jake what I should do. He said, "Read that prayer on the wall." It was a prayer for courage, but it didn't work.

At first I paced around the room while the patients were being prepared for surgery. Then I seated myself timidly on a stool in the corner while the surgeon did the operation. He removed two fingers and dropped them in a bucket. They dropped with a distinct clang and I felt sick. The surgeon asked me to join him in a demonstration on why the fingers had been removed. I tried to get up, but my legs wouldn't carry me. I felt quite ashamed of my cowardice and looked up at a picture of Mother Teresa. She looked so serene. I said to myself: If she can do this, so can I, and immediately I felt a great deal better. For the next operation I hovered nearby and by the end of the day I had won out over my fear.

The operating room consisted of three tables, all occupied with patients. When the first patient was wheeled out to the recovery ward, a new patient was placed on the table and I was asked to sit with him. I did and watched the next amputation. After the tea break, I decided to move closer to the operating table. I stood in awe as I watched the surgery. How easy it looked, yet how much skill it required. By lunch time fifteen amputations had been done, and three minor operations.

After lunch, two more amputations and two major operations were scheduled. One was a leg amputation and

I was utterly amazed at the flimsy saw that the surgeon used. It looked like an ordinary jigsaw. I feared it might break anytime. Unexpectedly the surgeon handed me the saw, indicating he wanted me to continue the sawing. Had it not been for the poor quality of the saw, I might have taken him up on it for by this time I'd become quite brave. When he had sawed a little longer he asked, as if it was the most normal thing in the world: "Please hold the leg up, will you?" When he'd severed the last tendon, I was left holding the leg. I wondered what to do with it, and was told to drop it in the bucket. With a thud, the leg hit the bucket. The eeriness of it all made me shiver.

The last operation was on a young man with major burns on the top part of his body. He was the only patient who received ether to knock him out. All the others had been given a local or spinal anaesthetic. Whenever this patient started to come around, the sister who stood at his head would pour more ether down the mask. According to Anna, who was a nurse, such a procedure hadn't been used in the West for twenty-five years. At the side of the bed, Father Jake held the arm that was being separated from the man's body. In the heat of the fire, the arm had melted onto the side of the body and this operation was to detach the arm. When the arm was separated at chest level, we could see the man's exposed heart. Once again, I felt squeamish. After the arm had been separated, skin was grafted from the man's leg and put on the open wound. I was overwhelmed. So many new experiences.

At dinner, Father Jake shared what his major experience had been that day. He told us that as he was holding the burn patient's arm, the patient kept resisting. Father had to struggle with him the whole time. While this was going on, Father imagined that this was what it must have been like when they tried to nail Christ on the cross. The patient and Christ would have been about the same age, and both were strong. Father Jake suspected that Christ, too, would have put up a struggle. Father was deeply moved by having an experience similar to the one the soldiers at the crucifixion must have had almost two thousand years ago.

After dinner, Anna bade us farewell as she was catching a night train to Calcutta. The three of us had had many wonderful discussions during and after meals; I knew I would miss her. That evening I went to the recovery ward, where some of the young boys from Boys Town were having a great time watching the fire victim struggle to get his arm loose. The arm had been tied to the bed to keep it from attaching itself back to his side. I went over to the poor man and sat for a while beside him. It was hard to say if he knew I was there. The next morning, to my surprise, he was sitting up in bed smiling. We tried to communicate. I thought he was telling me that he was disappointed they hadn't operated on his face as well. I tried to explain that he was scheduled to have three other operations. As we made a great effort to communicate, our eyes locked, and all of a sudden I was sure that we understood each other perfectly.

~

During my stay at Shanti Nagar, I was invited to one wedding and was privileged to be present at the negotiations for two others. For each girl, Mother Teresa provided a small dowry consisting of a few pots and pans, utensils, a blanket and a small amount of money. I had been to a few Indian weddings before, just because I was curious. I would walk in, help myself to food or the dessert buffet, and watch the entertainment, which consisted mostly of dancing. City weddings also often featured someone — usually the father of the bride or the father of the groom — bragging about the cost of the wedding. Weddings were certainly elaborate affairs with live bands, fancy saris, flowers and decorations every-where, and mountains of food.

The groom at the Shanti Nagar wedding had met his future bride when he worked as a construction worker at the settlement. He mustered up enough courage to talk with Sister Superior about a possible wedding. The sister gave him permission to have his family start negotiating with her family. Why Sister Superior was involved, I was not sure, but perhaps it was that the bride, as well as her parents, worked in the hospital. Neither the bride nor the groom had leprosy but their parents did.

The groom arrived from another state with his family. They filled two buses, but for the last three miles, they disembarked to walk and dance and shout and explode fireworks. When they finally reached the compound, the groom's representative offered gifts of clothes to the bride, her mother, and grandmother. I asked an English-speaking volunteer to explain in detail what was happening. He said that had the clothes not been accepted, the wedding might have been called off, or at least re-negotiated. It was a tense moment until the bride, her mother and grandmother sent the OK.

To me, both bride and groom looked about twelve years old, but my translator told me that they were seventeen. He added that child marriages were no longer legal, but still happened frequently because India did not have a marriage registry system.

The groom's party had arrived late. The sisters asked that the ceremony start so they could leave — they had to get to bed since they started their days so early. I noticed that they were enjoying the wedding as much as anyone. Their comments were like any other I had heard at weddings: "Isn't her sari beautiful?" and "Isn't the groom handsome in his wedding finery?" By this time, however, the groom's party was demanding to be fed. In fact, they insisted that unless they were fed, they would leave! There was much shouting, and finally the decision to proceed with the wedding was left in the hands of the groom's father. He deliberated the question for about an hour. I could feel the tension in the air. When he gave the agreed signal (I didn't know what the signal was), the wedding was on and everyone was able to relax for a while. This was not the only crisis. As the evening proceeded, frequently someone else's nose would get out of joint, and a new spat would have to be resolved.

The food served was the usual rice, vegetables and dahl — plain but plentiful. After the boy's family had been fed, the long ceremony started. First, the bride sat in the lap of her mother and was fed a few drops of milk. She repeated the process with her grandmother, signifying that the mother-daughter relationship was ending, and she would now belong to a new family. Following that part of the ceremony, a priest took over and chanted numerous prayers, all the while stoking a small fire. At 1:00 a.m., with the ceremonies complete, the party started. I went home, because I was leaving for New Delhi in a few hours. The next morning, as I walked through the gate of the Shanti Nagar complex, the two buses that had brought the groom's wedding party were just leaving. The band and the wedding party were still whooping it up. I was invited to join the party, and climbed on the roof of the bus with the band for the three-mile ride to my bus stop. The bride did not appear to be very happy — I guessed that she was dead tired from the preparations and the all-night partying.

~

When I wasn't working at Shanti Nagar, I spent many hours sitting on Pope Paul Boulevard. I chatted with the passers-by, watched the simple and peaceful life of the community, played with the babies and toddlers, and teased the teenagers. One day while I sat outside, three white women came walking up the road with luggage in hand. I went out to greet them, and found out we had new guests. I wondered what had happened to the rule of not mixing different genders. Two of the women were from Sweden and one from Germany. They intended to stay for only four days. After our first dinner together, I noticed how happy I was that I had some new and exciting people to talk with. We talked up such a storm that evening that one of the sisters came by to suggest we go to bed as we were making too much noise.

On Sunday after lunch, we managed to get five bikes and rode off into the countryside. After dinner that evening, the two Swedish women were writing letters. I asked who they were writing and both said that the letters were for their parents. I digested that information for a while, then asked them why they were writing home. In turn they responded: "Don't you?" I answered, "No, I never have." They thought that was rather strange. I had met others who liked to write and share their experiences with folks at home. For many years, I had wondered why my attitude was different.

Since the women were busy with their writing, I decided to go to bed early. But when I got to bed, my mind started going round and round about why I never wanted to write home. I kept tossing and turning in bed. Finally I found the answer. The next evening when we were talking, I broached the subject of living in the moment. We all agreed that was desirable and difficult to achieve. I shared with them what I had discovered for myself the previous night —that when I was away, particularly in India, I didn't want to think of home, but apply myself totally to the task at hand. Everyone said they were very impressed with my position, but weren't going to change their patterns. I stressed that I wasn't trying to change their habits. It just felt good for me to understand why I was different, and why this worked well for me.

In my last days at Shanti Nagar, I was introduced to changing bandages and putting salve on open wounds. I realized that I was looking forward to more volunteering in the medical field. At the end of my last Mass, Father Jake acknowledged our friendship publicly. I sat and cried with the recognition. During my stay, I had learned many things, but above all, I had learned how to give and receive pure unconditional love. The relationship between the sisters and all the staff and patients had been an example to me. I thirsted to have more and more experiences with this wonderful kind of love.

Chapter 17

~

Shishu Bhavan

The Missionaries of Charity organization has several homes for children, and over the years, I volunteered at three of them. Shishu Bhavan (Children's Home) in Calcutta was located just two blocks from Mother House, headquarters of the Missionaries of Charity. Since I was a frequent visitor to Mother House, I dropped in at Shishu Bhavan in Calcutta more frequently than at the other children's homes.

Shishu Bhavan was a large complex serving all kinds of functions besides being a home for children. In the courtyard, meals and health care were dispensed to the poor of Calcutta. Most of the day there were long queues of people. Trucks and ambulances went in and out constantly, delivering and picking up supplies such as food, medicine and clothes. The children were housed in two separate buildings: one for older children and another only for babies. Generally, as in all of the children's homes, Western volunteers were allowed to work only with the older children — the baby section was out of bounds.

One time, at Shishu Bhavan in Howrah, I was allowed to spend a few hours with the babies. I sat in the midst of twenty babies, each wanting to play, cuddle, or be recognized in some way. I spent two hours trying to keep them happy. While they had their diapers changed, I went for a tea break. Reeking of urine, I sat on the roof, basking in the warm sunshine, sipping my tea, and quietly weeping tears of overwhelming love for these beautiful and innocent children.

~

On my 1996 trip to Calcutta, my friend, Mary-Ellen Moore from New Hampshire, asked if I would join her in working in the adoption office at Shishu Bhavan in Calcutta. I did not hesitate.

The adoption office was the same as Mother Teresa's other facilities in that everything was basic. No fax machine, no computer, no modern office equipment, just a number of old desks, some ancient file cabinets and a manual typewriter. The office was made up of two sections. The front section was where three sisters worked, and the rear section was for Mary-Ellen and me. I liked this arrangement because it gave Mary-Ellen and me an opportunity to visit while we worked.

Our main function was to answer correspondence and do the filing. The mail mostly consisted of the annual reports required from the parents of each adopted child. We also received requests for adoptions. One such letter was from an Indian woman who wrote: "I am going to have a baby girl on October tenth, and it is urgent that I deliver a baby boy instead of a girl. Therefore if you could meet me behind the local grocery store October tenth with a baby boy we could exchange babies. If I don't deliver a boy my husband will kill me, so it most urgent that you meet me there."

Desperate parents from all over the world sent touching letters requesting babies. One mother who had given up her baby for adoption twenty years previously wrote to say her circumstances had changed and now she wanted to rescind the adoption. The majority of the adoptions were handled by two private agencies — one in Belgium and the other in Italy. Adoptions required a vast amount of paper work and were more efficiently processed by people familiar with the requirements.

My work was the filing of the annual reports and photographs from the new parents. At first I couldn't resist looking at all the photographs and reading the reports. I had tears in my eyes almost all day. What instigated some of my emotion was the memory of the day when my granddaughter, Samantha, came into my family's life, also through an adoption process. She was desperately wanted, as were all these children whose reports I was recording. One photograph was of a young healthy-looking girl in a ski parka. She was standing on a snowy mountain in Switzerland. Her dark, smiling face peeked out from her hood. I wondered what would have been her fate had she grown up in Calcutta. One thing was for sure — Calcutta had no ski slopes!

I loved to read the stories of scholastic achievements, or sports excellence, and the never-ending gratitude and pride of the adopting parents. The three weeks doing this work left me once again in awe of Mother Teresa's accomplishments.

Mary-Ellen had established a relationship with Sister Rani, who was in charge of the baby section, and as a result, we had visiting privileges. Sister Rani was the most inspiring sister I had ever met. Her loving and caring for her little charges was legendary. The story went that when Mother Teresa wished to talk with Sister Rani, she would go to her, rather than the (more usual) other way around. For many years, Sister Rani carried a pouch around her neck in which she would carry a baby needing twenty-four-hour-a-day care.

Each time I visited the baby ward, I found Sister Rani in the incubator room. To her joy, someone had recently donated eight incubators, and she needed every one. Some of the staff of the local hospitals were supplying Sister Rani with babies that had been aborted at a very late stage of the pregnancy. The staff would either deliver the babies to Sister Rani or phone her to collect them. Before then, they had thrown the live fetuses in the garbage. Some weighed as little as eight hundred grams. Legend had it that every one of them survived with Sister Rani's loving care.

On a tour of the huge ward, Sister Rani gave a running commentary on the history of each baby. The stories were brief but tragic: mother died in child birth; parents too poor or ill to care for a child; baby found floating in rain-filled gutter; child left on our door-step; unwed mother; baby simply unwanted. If a girl found herself pregnant and was not able to keep the child, Mother Teresa would take her in and provide care for her until she delivered her baby. She would then be encouraged to keep the baby, but if she chose not to, Mother Teresa was given legal custody of the baby. Some babies were never adopted and re-mained in the custody of Mother Teresa until they became adults. During that time, they obtained an education and most eventually got married.

◦

Mother Teresa's position on birth control and abortion was unacceptable to some. While working for her, I chose not to get involved in the controversy. I did admire Mother Teresa because she was unwavering in her position on the value of human life, and was always faithful to her beliefs and to her understanding of God. I absolutely believed that Mother Teresa did not have any personal agenda or thirst for fame — her only desire was to serve God and the poor. And I honoured that in her.

Section 4

≈

India

Chapter 18

∽

Sudder Street

I have heard Calcutta referred to as "the city of dreadful night"; I have also heard it referred to as "the city of love." Having lived in Calcutta off and on for a total of over twelve months, I find that both descriptions fit, but my experience has been that the hardship existing there has made it a loving place. I first found Sudder Street through my *Lonely Planet* guide book, and it became by far my favourite place to stay in Calcutta. Sudder Street was where I discovered the heart beating under all the filth of the city. When I became willing to surrender my need for comfort and cleanliness, I awakened my compassion and discovered wonderful lessons in tolerance and patience.

∽

Sure, Sudder Street was somewhat noisy, and a bit dirty, and the hotels and restaurants had some flaws, but it was home to me. The area consisted of budget hotels and restaurants and small shops, and tourists were in the majority. Of the hotels, my first choice was the Modern

Lodge, which wasn't modern, but was reasonably clean. On the second floor, there was a lounge with some comfortable furniture, also a roof-top garden where most of the Sudder Street parties took place. I preferred the roof-top rooms, although they tended to be noisy with the parties. My room cost about 200 rupees, one of the highest rates on the street, but it included a bathroom, and that was important to me.

My hotel was near a fire station built in 1923. I was sure that the firefighters still used the same equipment they had then. The firetrucks were ancient and slow-moving; often the snarled traffic prevented them from moving at all. A few of the firetrucks had a bell mounted on the cab. One firefighter would sit in the cab and either pound the bell with a hammer or furiously pull a cord attached to the hammer inside the bell. Every time I saw this sight, I thought of the Keystone Cops I watched on TV as a child.

My favourite restaurant was the Blue Sky Café. It was here that I made most of my social contacts and ate almost all of my meals. The café was small and always crowded, but to me had a homey feeling. I whiled away many hours there listening to travel stories and sharing experiences with other travellers.

Sudder Street was a safe place to live. Many of the residents were volunteers with various organizations in Calcutta, and some had lived there for years. But not everyone liked this street. On one of my visits, I was helping guide a group of tourists around Calcutta. I looked forward to showing them my home and organized a tour of Sudder Street for them. Only their group leader finished the tour — all the others escaped back to the comfort of their deluxe coach. During the tour, it was clear that the leader's experience was quite different from mine. He walked around a mangy dog lying on the sidewalk and said that it looked like it was dying — how gross. (I patted the dog and sent it love.) He wanted to rush past five families camped near the Salvation Army hostel — the children were so dirty. (I greeted them, they greeted me, and I watched the children playing a game.) He complained that the aggressive beggars were a nuisance. (I said hello to my friends.) He said that the food stalls were smelly and filthy. (To me the food smelled good.) He said that the hotel was dirty, he had to fight my way through the laundry hanging on clothes lines, the room was small, the paint was peeling, and there was no toilet seat. (I would have described it as: laundry is conveniently outside room, there is a toilet, and the room is cosy.) Yes, were in the same place!

At home on Sudder Street, 1995

I came to know most of the people on Sudder Street. One day, a chap who had never begged before asked me for 10 rupees to help burn one of the street people. At first, I didn't believe his story. He responded by showing me the dead man on a sidewalk one street over. I gave him 10 rupees, and asked how much he needed to raise. He said, "About 400." I decided to help him raise the money. As we walked down the street together, I asked each Westerner for a 10-rupee donation, and everyone I asked donated. He solicited the Indians, choosing everyone except the beggars and the rickshaw pullers, but they came forward voluntarily to make donations anyway. It was a most heart-warming experience. In about thirty minutes, we had raised 600 rupees. With the extra he said he would buy some flowers and incense.

One night, Abduhl, a rickshaw puller, called me over.

"You don't like me, do you?" he said.

"Where did you get an idea like that?" I asked.

"You have been coming here for years and you have never said hello to me," he said. I explained that Westerners were asked constantly for money by beggars and rickshaw pullers. For me, it wasn't a matter of disliking, but of surviving. I wasn't sure if he believed me, or whether that made sense to him, but we ended up having a pleasant chat. He told me that he was from the state of Bihar. His family, including his wife, three boys and two girls, still lived there. Every two months or so, he went to visit them. He and twelve other men, all from Bihar, lived in Stewart Lane just off Sudder Street. There they parked their rickshaws and slept on the sidewalk.

I was touched by his story and every night when I came out of the Blue Sky Café, I stopped to talk with him for a few moments. Sometimes I commiserated with him when he had had a bad day, and had not made enough money to cover the rickshaw rental payment for the day.

Rickshaw puller on Sudder Street, 1995.
Calcutta is the only place in India where these human horses still exist.

And from then on, I chatted to rickshaw pullers whenever possible.

My best friend on the street was Chico, who had been a waiter at the Blue Sky Café for twelve years. When I first met him, he used to make only 20 rupees a day, starting at 6:00 a.m. and finishing at 10:00 p.m., and he slept on a table in the restaurant. He loved his job, and was very good at it. Over the years, his income rose to 32 rupees a day and he had afternoons off. His wife lived back in his village, and he went there every May for one month. On his time off, he found a quiet place on the street to sleep or worked at maintaining the Hindu shrine outside the restaurant. We shopped together many times — he knew where the bargains were.

A group of Muslim taxi drivers on the street were always buying me tea. During Ramadan (thirty days of fasting every day until sunset), I had many meals with them. At that time, they were particularly generous. They often asked me for large loans, and I never granted them, but they were a great source of information about what was going on in town, and about how or where to find things.

Michael, the street drunk, was another friend. I heard his tale of woe often. When drunk he was abusive, so I only talked with him when he had run out of money and was sober. I encouraged him to seek help, and told him where support was available when he wanted it. Michael was not the only one on Sudder Street who had problems with drugs or alcohol. I took Valerie, a twenty-three-year-old drug addict, to a treatment centre a few times, but each time she stayed there only a few days. One lane off Sudder Street was a nightly gathering place for rag-pickers. I stood and watched many times while they shared one needle to shoot drugs, and between shots sucked on the needle to clean it. On two occasions, I saw them introducing young boys to the needle. I was horrified and screamed at them. This had absolutely no impact — they just stared at me in their euphoric state.

Many street kids made their home on Sudder Street. One fourteen-year-old boy, Phillip, spoke fluent English. He received a thousand rupees a month from a woman in Germany who had informally adopted him a few years earlier. Phillip lived in a small apartment and had no financial concerns, so he hung around the street, even begging sometimes. The last time I was in India, in 1997, I was happy to hear that he had gone into a program of rehabilitation with an organization called Don Bosco, where he would be taught a trade and any other living skills he might need. Unfortunately, he only stayed for one month because part of the program required him to work. In his words: "Why work? I have enough." It seemed to me that the kind woman from Germany was not doing him any favours. What would happen to him when she died or stopped sending money? Many other youngsters on the street tried the Don Bosco program. Like Phillip, their main objections were that they had to go to school and work or do chores. It was much easier to live on the street and hope to make it big like Phillip. What was tragic was that everybody lost — the kids were robbed of an opportunity to get their lives together, and the tourists sooner or later discovered that they were being fleeced.

Frequently I saw well-meaning people pour heart and soul into another human being, trying to be another Mother Teresa, only to discover that they had certain expectations. When these expectations weren't met, they were devastated. For example, one couple I knew gave money for medicine only to learn it had been spent on booze. Yet they found it difficult to say no next time. For me, Mother Teresa was an example in this as in so many other things. She did say no — in fact, I had to say no many times on her behalf. For instance, there was a man who would check into the facility once a week and want to be discharged after a few days. At that time, the person being discharged received a blanket. This particular man made a living selling the blankets he acquired this way. When Mother Teresa realized what he was doing, she told us to stop giving him blankets.

∾

With all of its diversified characters, its dogs, cats, goats, rats, children, and adults, Sudder Street is full of colours, smells, smiles, frowns, caring, sharing, anger, and fear. It's where West and East meet and are blended. It's my idea of heaven.

Chapter 19

∼

Christmas in Calcutta

This chapter is about one Christmas I spent in Calcutta. I didn't miss the hustle and bustle that goes along with the Christmas season in North America, where there is great abundance of material wealth, but not so much of the emotional and spiritual wealth that I thirst for. I look forward to spending more and more Christmases in a country such as India where the thirst for self-gratification is not as predominant as it is in the West. I seek a simple life with a focus on transformation of self leading naturally to the transformation of the planet. To me, that's what the Christmas message is all about.

∼

It was Christmas Eve in Calcutta, and about three hundred people were jammed into the courtyard of the Sudder Street Salvation Army hostel. I just managed to get inside. Many did not get in and crowded into the street. With the Salvation Army band enthusiastically playing Christmas carols, everyone was in the Christmas spirit. Most sang along with the band. Some sang in the language of their home country. The couple next to me held each other around the waist and fought back tears as they sang "Stille Nacht, Heilige Nacht." I embraced my co-worker, Guissepi from Italy. As he hugged me in return, we wished each other a Merry Christmas, I in my Canadian accent and he in his Italian accent.

Word spread that it was time to move on. The band stopped playing, and the band major quickly dispersed some of the band members to pass the hat in support of the work of the Salvation Army. The whole group slowly started to snake down Sudder Street. Life in Calcutta was constantly disrupted by protest marches and demonstrations, but rarely did they occur at night. Someone familiar with life in Calcutta might have asked: What was this strange group doing on December 24 at ten o'clock at night? Most groups marching in Calcutta carried huge red banners with arm-and-sickle emblems signifying an association with one of the many Communist parties in the state of West Bengal. Instead of banners, this group was carrying lit candles. Led by two guitarists, one trumpet player and a violinist, this group was not shouting slogans, but singing songs. No speeches, no stern faces, just smiles and voices singing. Another major difference was that these were faces of Westerners, not Indians.

As we moved down the street, many participants walked up to complete strangers and cheerfully called out: "Merry Christmas!" The sidewalk dwellers were awakened by the noise, and stared at us bleary-eyed from beneath their flimsy blankets. The young and industrious urchins who made a living on the streets were delighted to have their sleep disturbed. Instantly they went to work begging for a meal, a few rupees, a shirt, or a pair of pants. A taxi slowly crept up the street through the jubilant crowd, the driver smiling and returning greetings. Another motorist simply gave up trying to drive in the street. He and his family climbed on the roof of their car and enjoyed watching the happy crowd. For most of the route, automobile traffic waited patiently for the procession to pass, but once in a while a disgruntled motorist would force his way through, leaning on his horn the whole time. But the spirit of this throng wasn't affected. Slow-moving streetcars were invaded by the revellers loudly singing "We Three Kings of Orient Are."

The procession wound through the narrow side streets of Calcutta, stopping to give impromptu concerts outside a boys' home, a jail, a seniors' home, and the homes of various friends. Ninety minutes later, we reached Mother House, the headquarters of the Missionaries of Charity. We were greeted by large number of beggars who knew about this annual event and decided to make it a productive evening for themselves. Their persistence made it difficult to enter Mother House. At one point, Mother Teresa herself came out to ask the beggars to give way.

Inside, we jammed into the first-floor courtyard to perform a Christmas pageant. Baby Jesus was an unhappy Indian baby who wailed the whole time he was in the manger. His mother, Mary, was played by a blonde woman from Sweden, and Joseph, his father, by an American. It was a real United Nations! With the pageant complete, all went to the second-floor chapel for the traditional Roman Catholic midnight Mass. I left after ten minutes as I was bored and wanted to spend time with my ailing partner who had stomach flu.

≈

On Christmas Day, I went to work as usual at Kalighat, Mother Teresa's home for the dying and destitute. For the past week, a number of volunteers had spent all their time repairing and making new Christmas decorations. Now streamers were hanging from the rafters, bows hung above the windows, and a nativity scene adorned the area between the men's section and the pharmacy. The pictures on the walls were surrounded by angel hair, and a huge electrically lit star was mounted on the roof. At night the star was awesome — it even lit up the Hindu symbols on the Kali temple.

The Christmas spirit started first thing in the morning when the patients were dressed in fine quality, pink bedclothes, instead of the usual coarse cloth many times mended. With the new clothes, the energy of the whole

Male patients' ward at Kalighat, Christmas 1995

room was transformed, and the patients' happiness spread throughout the building. To add to the happiness and excitement, around ten o'clock Mother Teresa made an appearance. She stayed for several hours, chatting with everyone, giving blessings and being herself. She spread joy and happiness so naturally.

A group I worked with had been preparing a Christmas program for patients and staff. To my disappointment, instead of doing something original, the sister superior had insisted on yet another nativity play. I was to play the part of John the Baptist. My roommate had made me a gorgeous costume out of a tablecloth. I looked magnificent, I thought. I had been to many pageants, but this was the first time I had been anything but an observer. I was also conscripted into working in the kitchen to prepare Christmas dinner. In the afternoon, all the male patients were moved into one corner of the women's ward and we performed our pageant. The patients enjoyed the change in routine if not the show itself.

Later that day, one of the major hotels put on a Christmas gathering for its clients and I had received an invitation. I had to buy a shirt with a collar for the occasion, since I had only T-shirts with me. I was still underdressed, as there was only one other man without a jacket. This function reminded me of many Christmases in the past, all those Christmases of too much booze and food, and relatives discontented with their gifts or disillusioned with life in general. Luckily, I had already experienced the best of Christmases at Kalighat.

Chapter 20

~

Trains

I have a passion for trains and have always wanted to see how they are built. This desire led to one of my most pleasant adventures in India. I tried many times to gain access to a large locomotive factory in Chittyranjan. Foreigners were refused entry into the plant, but I was determined to get in. I planned my attack while cycling around the factory. The cyclist I was following turned into the gate and nodded at the guard without stopping. I followed the cyclist, nodded at the guard, and kept on pedalling. I spent three delightful hours treating myself to a tour.

That was the only time I've been able to see how trains are built, but I have spent a lot of time on them. Since the distances are so great in Canada and the United States, I rarely use the trains there, but they are my preferred method of travel in Europe. I have also travelled extensively on the trains in India. India Rail is one hundred and forty-three years old. In 1989, the last time I collected statistics, it was the world's largest employer with one million, six hundred thousand employees. On my last trip to India, in 1997, the railway was still expanding at a phenomenal pace, with new routes opening almost weekly.

Train travel in India can be challenging, starting with the purchase of the ticket. In the major centres, foreign tourists can purchase tickets in special offices, which saves an average of four hours in a line-up. Although the trains are scheduled to run frequently, they are rarely on time. The railway system is very inexpensive — in 1997, a sample fare for a twenty-four-hour train ride between New Delhi and Calcutta was U.S. $8.50, and that rate included a berth. While travelling by train in India is inexpensive, it is also far from clean or even comfortable. Many times I have thought that I should have elbow and knee pads, maybe a helmet, and a gas mask for the toilet!

In addition to long-distance trains, India Rail has many local trains. These have hard wooden benches, and are even more dilapidated than the long-distance trains I usually take. The overcrowding on the local trains is amazing to see. Passengers cling to every part of the train, and even bulge out of doorways. I suspect that very few people bother buying tickets since no control seems apparent. In and around train stations, the rat population is extremely high since a lot of food is discarded around the area. These rats don't fear humans. One time I was sitting on a bench in New Delhi station and fell asleep. When I awoke, there were rats all around me. I jumped up and did an insane dance, trying both to scare the rats away and to avoid stepping on them. The other passengers stared at me as though they couldn't understand what the fuss was all about.

~

The most frequent long-distance route I took was from New Delhi to Calcutta. From Calcutta I travelled to Puri, Varanasi, Chitaranjan, Pune, Titaghar, Gaya, and Bombay. The longest trip I ever took was forty-two hours and the shortest forty-five minutes.

On one typical trip, as the train pulled into the station, passengers began clambering aboard while it was still moving. When it stopped, the rest of the passengers charged the entrance. I had learned to stand and observe the chaos. When the crunch was over, I leisurely boarded the train knowing at the same time that I was going to create a huge scene. Even though my ticket reserved a berth for me, I knew from experience that most travellers grabbed whatever seats they could. When I found my seat, I asked the person occupying it to move. This caused a minor uproar in the coach, as always, but I wouldn't budge. By now most of the people in the coach were irritated with me. I heaved all the luggage off my top berth. Having settled myself comfortably up on my berth, I stretched out and read a book, ignoring the glances from the people around me. Throughout the trip, I tried to use the toilet as little as possible because it was smelly and dirty.

Overlooking the negative aspects of train travel, once I settled in my space I often got into interesting conversations with my fellow travellers. I especially enjoyed playing with the children. The train was a community on wheels. We all shared food. Many brought picnic baskets jammed full of goodies that made me drool. All day, food vendors travelled through the coach. I preferred to purchase food on the platform at stops, as it was fresher than the food sold on the train. My meals

Children outside Calcutta, 1996.
Wherever I went, children asked me:
"Take my picture, take my picture."

often consisted of eggs, either boiled or as an omelette, supplemented with oranges and bananas.

On another trip, my companion and I couldn't get second-class tickets so took first-class sleeper tickets at triple the cost (it wasn't worth it). I checked the listing pasted on the outside of the train to establish with whom we would be sharing the space. According to the listing, we would be joined by two males age fifty-four and forty-nine. I was determined not to be overcrowded since I was paying triple the cost of second class. My companion and I were the only occupants of the compartment when we left the station at Puri. Since this was a night train, we crawled into our bunks.

At the next stop, an older man entered the compartment with a young man who looked to be in his twenties. Since the only lights were from the station, it was difficult to see them, but I knew the young man did not belong there since he was obviously neither forty-nine nor fifty-four. I yelled at them to leave. The older man shone his flashlight on me, and said he was the conductor. I feared I might be kicked off the train for my belligerent attitude. The conductor explained that the original person hadn't shown up and this young fellow would now occupy that bunk. Embarrassed, I crawled back into my sleeping bag. Several stops later, a noisy group of about six people entered the compartment. They were disturbing my slumber and definitely had no business in the compartment, and I told them so, in a loud voice. One member of the group looked up at me and said, "These people are getting off. They are just escorting me to my berth." This time I was doubly embarrassed, for the man that spoke to me was wearing the orange robes of a holy man. I vowed to keep my mouth shut as I tucked myself back into my sleeping bag.

The next morning, the first person to rouse was the holy man. I could hear him stir, and knew that sooner or later I would have to face him. I turned over and peeked down at him. He looked up and greeted me with a very cheerful "Good morning." What a relief that he wasn't angry! He commented, "You obviously have travelled in India some, since you were protecting your space." He not only was amused but also approved! Now that it was safe to came out of my sleeping bag, I spent the rest of the trip having philosophical discussions with him.

On another occasion, after a harrowing bus trip from Bodgaya to Gaya in the state of Bihar, I arrived at the railway station and was told to stand in a certain line. After a one-hour wait, I learned that I was in the wrong line. This happened three times. Rather than explode in anger, I decided to go for a coffee in the hotel across the street. By the time I got back from coffee, they had cancelled two of the three trains leaving for Calcutta. I was assured that it was impossible to get a seat out of there that day. I was absolutely determined to get to Calcutta, and didn't want to stay in Gaya even one night.

At another counter, another passenger looked as though she was about to attack the ticket vendor sitting in his protective wire cage. I went over to see what was going on. She too did not want to stay in Gaya. She introduced herself as Hilly. She was twenty-eight and from Holland. We headed across the street to the restaurant I had just left, had dinner, and discussed our dilemma. She asked whether I had tried to get the tourist quota ticket — the number of seats reserved for tourists at each station. I had completely forgotten about that possibility.

After finishing our meal, we went back to the station and found the tourist office tucked in a back corner. The man in charge said that tourist seats were only held until 2:00 p.m. each day. Since it was seven o'clock by now, they were long gone, and we already knew that two trains had been cancelled. I realized that the situation was hopeless and grabbed my bag to leave. Hilly, however, was not to be deterred. She made the man have one more look at his records. He then said that maybe he could do something, but it would cost us 200 rupees each. Without consulting me, she said that we would take it. The 200 rupees was not to pay the fare, but was a bribe we were paying the tourist official as well as the conductor. While these negotiations were going on, the train arrived. We were given VIP treatment. We were escorted aboard the train and a number of people were told to vacate our seats and berth. We retired to our berths.

The hours of hassle had taken their toll. I fell asleep almost instantly and slept soundly until 6:30 a.m., when a man shook me awake. He said that I was in his bunk and that Hilly was in his wife's bunk. We had been sold someone else's seats! Once again, Hilly took the lead and refused to give up her berth, yelling and screaming about the corrupt Indian system. We got some sympathy from the man when we told him we had paid 500 rupees for these seats. He had paid only 150. After some negotiation, to which I was only an observer, Hilly and the man worked out a compromise: we would share the seats. Things worked out after all, but I didn't feel good about the bribe. Although it was a widespread practice in India, usually I felt I had I to take a stand against bribery and would go to any length to avoid such involvement. That particular night, however, I would have paid almost anything to get on that train.

Chapter 21

∽

Living on the Edge

I love excitement and the adrenaline rush that comes with it. I like living on the edge. I jaywalk while dodging fast-moving cars. When I reach the other side, I feel jubilant. I have asked others who jaywalk why they do it, and like me, about a third do it for the challenge. My most favourite road in the world to cross is Chowringhee Road in Calcutta. It's the only road in Calcutta where cars can actually work up some speed. The frustrated motorists take advantage of it and push their accelerators to the floor. A renowned dancer couldn't match my agility as I match my wits against the trucks and buses on that road. A sign that says Do Not Trespass beckons me to explore. As a result, I have been chased by dogs, confronted by security guards, and challenged by soldiers with rifles. Someday I would like to skydive or bungy jump.

∽

It was while talking with an eighty-year-old man from Ireland in a restaurant that I launched into one of my more exciting adventures in Calcutta. We were talking about a book we'd both read — Dominique Lapierre's *City of Joy* (New York: Warner Books, 1985). The book was centred around a slum in Calcutta, and one chapter described how an inhabitant of the slum arranged to sell his own dead body. When his death was imminent, there was a buyer eager and willing to pay one-third now and two instalments later for his remains.

I had found that section of the book particularly interesting, but hadn't given it much thought after that. With a twinkle in his eyes, my Irish friend told a fascinating story of how he and a young man from England had gone looking for the place where, according to the book, people went to find a purchaser for their bodies. He thought they had found the place, but a few things didn't fit. For one thing, in the book, the office used skulls for paperweights, and the place they found didn't. Also, when they had asked the man in charge if he was selling the bodies stored there, the man said: "No, that is illegal." When asked about the room with tables where bodies were being carved and flesh was being stripped from bones, the man said: "I am too busy and must get back to work."

My Irish friend was convinced that they had came across a very dubious bunch of fellows. Neither he nor the English chap would go back, he said, for the odour in the room had been overwhelming. I told him I was writing a book and asked him to direct me to the place so that I could see it for myself. He said he couldn't because he had had many a nightmare over what he had seen and the stench was such that he never wanted to smell it again. He desperately wanted to get more details on the office with the skulls, and was willing to assist me in any way he could, short of having to go back to that place himself.

His directions were vague, although I knew the area was in the northern part of the city. He was adamant — I should look for a hospital inside a fenced area with many buildings, and go the rear of the complex where there was a building with all its windows boarded up. He was sure that the windows were boarded up because something illegal was happening in there. And they were trying to keep nosy people like ourselves out. Of course, I was intrigued.

Right away, I went looking for the place he had described. I could hardly contain my excitement when I found a hospital complex. I was sure it was the right place. My Irish friend had said that the edifice I was looking for was to the rear of many other structures. I headed down a road with many buildings on either side. As I neared the end of this group of structures, I saw some workers in hospital whites smoking behind one of the buildings. They spotted me and one yelled: "Are you lost?" I was startled and my first thought was to run, but I was determined to get to the rear of those buildings. I pretended I hadn't heard him and kept walking calmly to my destination.

Behind the next building was another smoker who said, "Uncle, you are not supposed to be here!" What to do? Run? Keep walking? Or turn around? By now, my nerves were about to snap! While I was debating my next course of action, two men walked past me. They were supporting a bamboo pole on their shoulders. Hanging between them on the pole was a burlap sack with feet sticking out. As soon as I saw them, my decision was made: I was not leaving! The men were wearing the street clothing of the poor (lungis, which are made of one-metre lengths of cloth wrapped the waist around and tucked in).

Had they been wearing hospital uniforms or just about anything else, I wouldn't have noticed them. But they looked out of place here. Why would men wearing lungis rather than hospital uniforms be carrying a body wrapped in a burlap sack and not on a stretcher? This was positively it!

The men walked through an open door. I didn't have time to see if the windows were boarded up — I followed them through the door. Just inside the door, they dumped what I could now see was a female body onto the floor next to two male bodies already lying there. I quickly surveyed the room. A man was sitting at a desk to the left of me, and in front of me was an empty desk. Behind me was a huge pile of clothes, and on the right a doorway. I headed for the doorway and looked in. Many bodies were strewn about the room. Behind the bodies were shelves full of human parts. The man sitting at the desk finally noticed me and started to yell at me in an Indian language I didn't understand. I ignored him, and he came towards me.

When he was standing right next to me, I couldn't ignore him any longer and indicated that I wanted to have a look around the room. He told me with gestures that he needed a large bottle of alcohol. I decided that 10 rupees would buy him a bottle, and offered him 10 rupees. For some reason, that greatly offended him. He began waving his arms wildly and I thought it best to leave. Outside, I realized that I could hardly breathe, the stench was so strong. In all the excitement inside, I had hardly noticed the smell.

I was still tingling with excitement and was determined to go back with a bottle of alcohol to appease the man in charge. When I got back to my street, I went into the same restaurant where I had met my Irish friend. As luck would have it, he was eating his dinner. I breathlessly recounted my story. He was as enthusiastic as I was until he asked me what the name of the hospital was. I told him, and he said that I was at the wrong place because the hospital he'd found had either "Calcutta" or "City" in its name. He asked me if I had seen the skulls on a desk. I thought about it and said yes, I had seen some on the vacant desk. Since I hadn't found the room full of tables and the body carvers, I couldn't convince him that I had found the right place. Also, I wasn't sure whether the windows on the building had been boarded up. Because the man in charge had reacted so violently, I was sure I had found the right place, and decided to establish proof by going back that evening. I made a mental list of the items to look for.

When I got to the hospital much later, the first thing I looked for was the words "Calcutta" or "City" on the board outside. No such luck. I headed down the road towards the back of the complex. Most of the buildings were not lit inside or out, but the moonlight was adequate to see the building outlines and to establish whether or not the windows were covered. My heart was racing with excitement and I was clammy with perspiration for fear of being discovered. I realized that I was possibly in danger walking around an area where illegal activity was taking place. I questioned my sanity for being there so late at night and in such darkness. I jumped when out of the shadows a stern voice hailed me. As the man came closer and noticed my white skin, he mellowed and seemed to relax about my being there.

"No English. Bengali?" he said. I understood him to mean that he didn't speak English, but did speak Bengali.

"Nay Bengali," I said, indicating that I couldn't speak Bengali. "Can I look inside?" I pointed to the structure I had been in earlier that day. He shrugged, indicating his consent, and seemed puzzled by my request. He led the way and flicked on the light switch. On the floor, at the door where the three bodies had been earlier, now there was only one, a very obese male naked from the waist up and with a huge scar from his navel to his upper chest. On the desk where I had seen skeletons, there weren't any. The smell was so horrendous I had to get out of there. But first I had to find the door that led to the laboratory. I couldn't see one. I looked through the doorway on the right, where the room full of bodies had been earlier. The room was now bare. I thought, Aha! they have hidden the evidence!

The room had no exit doors. My Irish friend must have been mistaken about the laboratory. I thanked my guide, gave him 5 rupees, and left. Then I continued my search for boarded-up windows. Three buildings away, a light beamed out from an open door. I decided to investigate. The lone man inside was spreading a blanket on the floor. It looked as though he was ready to go to bed. I walked into the room and said hello. He just stared blankly. I surmised that he didn't speak English and pointed to the door behind him, indicating I wanted to go in there. He said, "Nay." They must be hiding something, I thought, and offered him 5 rupees to show me behind the door. That took care of his objection. He opened the door and showed me a room with thirty stacked refrigerators.

I asked him to open one of the refrigerators and an empty drawer slid out. Obviously these were for bodies. Still searching for the door to the alleged laboratory, I went completely around the room. There was no door, but

I felt I was getting close in my search. I thanked the man, and went on looking for those boarded-up windows. I checked all the structures in the complex with no success. As I was leaving the complex, I saw a sign that I hadn't noticed before. It was a map of the complex. After I had studied it in detail, I realized that the building with the bodies was labelled Morgue and the building with the refrigerators was marked Anatomy Department. They weren't hiding anything after all. I felt very let down. Obviously, my Irish friend was mistaken.

Most of the next day I was grinning at myself, amused with how my passion for excitement had led me on such a wild goose chase. Again I had been carried away with my wild imagination. Two days later, the waiter in the restaurant told me that my Irish friend was looking for me. I asked the waiter to pass on the message that I would meet my friend for dinner at six o'clock. My Irish friend arrived at six and announced: "I have good news for you! The place you're looking for is not two blocks past the newspaper office, but two miles." His memory had been jogged, he said. I told him I was finished playing detective and wouldn't go. (I had decided he was senile.) He insisted that was the place and tried pressure: "The readers of your book have to know the truth." I protested, "I know the area and there is no hospital there." He stormed over to the restaurant cashier and asked about a hospital in that area. The cashier said the only thing near there was the Calcutta medical school. "That's it! That's it!" he shouted. Realizing that the medical school did have the word "Calcutta" in it, I gave in and agreed to go.

The next day, I headed for the medical school with great anticipation. This could be it! This complex had a fence around it — a good sign. The next thing I looked for was the building with the boarded-up windows. About halfway through my search, I saw a sign: Body Donations Office Upstairs. My adrenalin was really flowing. At last I had found it! I went up a flight of stairs into an office and said to the woman there that I wanted to donate my body. She handed me a form to complete. I said, "Before I complete this form, how much will you pay for my body?" She said, "We don't pay. The sign says donate." I asked where I could go to get paid for my body, and she said there was no such thing. I believed her.

Discouraged, I left the office. At the bottom of the stairs was a closed door. I decided to try it, and inside found a room filled with tables. The blanket over the third one on the right looked as though it might be covering a body. A crowd was gathered around two other tables. I went to investigate. These tables were surrounded by medical students watching professors demonstrating surgical techniques. The back wall was filled with floor-to-ceiling shelves containing large jars of body parts floating in a clear liquid.

Later that day, I met with my Irish friend and gave him my latest report. I also told him I had given up the pursuit. He wasn't pleased, and felt slighted. He thought that I didn't believe him. I told him that in two days I would be leaving Calcutta and didn't have time to pursue the matter any further.

~

I already feel excited about my next adventure. Recently I was thumbing through a book about the world's most dangerous places. I haven't bought it . . . yet. I thirst for the next challenge to come my way, and most of all for the growth that is the inevitable result. Not being overly fearful has helped me cope with many day-to-day issues. I no longer worry much — I can't do much about the future and the past is over. For me, living on the edge is living in the moment.

Chapter 22

~

Travel Stories

People often ask me for tips about travelling in India. My first suggestion is to buy *The Lonely Planet*, a travel book published in Australia by Lonely Planet Publications. They publish books for travel everywhere, and cover every detail of travel. My second suggestion is simply to do it! People also often ask me for stories about travelling in India. Some of my favourite tidbits are in this chapter.

Ladakh

Two different people had recommended two books on Ladakh and that was enough of a reason to check it out. I read both books — carefully, I thought — and learned that Ladakh was a district in the state of Jammu and Kashmir, located on a high plateau in the most northerly portion of India. I concluded that my next trip to India would include a visit to Leh in Ladakh.

After arriving at my Calcutta hotel on my next trip, I told my Bangladesh neighbours that I was leaving for Leh. They warned me about the high altitude.

"Yes, I know," I replied. "I will be close enough to shake hands with God." Their fourteen-year-old son was listening intently, and a while later came to me with a puzzled and troubled look.

"What are you going to say to God?" he asked. I didn't know why he was so troubled, and thought it best to explain that I wasn't really going to shake hands with God. He seemed to be relieved. I later wished I had questioned him about his interest in this topic.

When I arrived at the airport in Leh, I was expecting the high altitude, but not the temperature, which was well below freezing. While I waited for my luggage, I read a large sign in the terminal that said the altitude was over fifteen thousand feet and suggested that newcomers go to bed for the first twenty-four hours to avoid altitude sickness. Standing next to me was a young woman, also reading the sign. I hadn't seen her on the airplane. I asked her if she knew how far it was to town, but she didn't know. I suggested we share a taxi, and that was agreeable to her. We checked into the same hotel, the only one open out of fifty. We arranged to meet for dinner that evening, after we had had a chance to rest and adjust somewhat to the altitude. She had a guide book and had selected several restaurants, but all her selections were closed for the season. After much searching we found a restaurant that was open. Just two dishes were available: an egg omelette or a bowl of noodles.

As we ate, we shared our concern that we might freeze to death that night. Our first impression was: Let's get out of here! Back at the hotel, we found out how to contact Indian Airlines office the next day in order to rearrange our flights. We asked where we could have breakfast in the morning. The owner said nothing would be open, but we could eat with his family. That turned out to be a most pleasant experience. The food was good, and his family hospitable. The earliest we could get a flight out was in three days. Each day the owner suggested what sights to see. We went to a total of six monasteries, all well worth visiting. At the end of the three days, I decided to return for another visit — next time in warmer weather.

Shey Monastery, Leh, Ladakh, 1997

Spontaneity

While I was sitting in the Leh airport waiting for a flight to New Delhi, I heard an announcement that the plane sitting on the tarmac was not going to New Delhi until later that evening. It had been redirected to Jammu, located in the southern part of the state of Jammu and Kashmir. I had never been there, and asked if it was possible to go to Jammu instead of New Delhi. The clerk said not only that I could but that I would receive a lower fare. The young woman I had met in Leh wanted to go to Jammu as it was close to Dharamsala, where the Dali Lama lived, but was afraid of going into that part of Kashmir since there was a lot of unrest there. She decided to wait for the flight to New Delhi. I decided to go to Jammu.

I informed the desk clerk that I was going to Jammu, and he re-issued my tickets. I was bused to the Boeing 737. At the gangway, the steward said I was a VIP since I was the only passenger on the flight. On the fifty-minute trip, I was even served a meal. At Jammu, a small crowd was standing on the runway, and applauded when I came down the stairs. They must have thought I was a visiting dignitary.

I realized I didn't know anything about Jammu. I inquired about items of local interest and received the impression that there weren't any. I decided to take a train to Dharamsala from Jammu, and found the railway station, but was informed that there were no trains to Dharamsala. Buses did go there, however, so I asked for directions for the bus depot. I was told numerous times that there were no buses to Dharamsala, but I persisted, and finally got on a bus to Dharamsala. Two hours later, the bus stopped and the driver motioned me to get off. The sign didn't say Dharamsala so I wouldn't get off. The bus driver and the rest of the passengers were getting annoyed with me, but I wasn't moving. The driver went in search of someone to talk English to me. The man he found explained that I had to transfer to another bus. I got off the bus and waited for the next one. Three hours later the same situation occurred again, and again I insisted I wasn't getting off the bus until I reached my destination. A passenger on the bus came to my rescue and arranged for a rickshaw to take me to the next town and my final bus. After a gruelling twenty hours, I arrived at Dharamsala at 3:00 a.m.

The next day, I went to see the Dali Lama and the area around his palace. Sometimes I questioned my thirst to be spontaneous, but mostly the results were worthwhile.

Goodwill Tour

Each year an Indian friend of mine who is also a Mother Teresa volunteer received a parcel from a woman in Germany. It contained perhaps fifty hand-sewn garments to be distributed to the poor. One year my friend chose to distribute the clothes in the Sunderbans, a group of small islands at the mouth of the Ganges River. He recruited four Western volunteers to join him. We travelled two hours by bus, then took two ferries and arrived just before lunch at our destination.

At the ferry, several local dignitaries greeted us and took us by taxi to the village. From there we walked through the countryside with an entourage of a hundred or so people following. The dignitaries led us to a mud house and served a delicious lunch, then we were once again paraded through the fields to a local village to inspect the new library. After that, we were whisked away from the throngs to our guest house, to unpack and relax. That evening, we were guests of honour at the local fair ground. Five thousand people showed up to see us. We spent several hours on a stage listening to speeches and each of us Westerners was asked to bring greetings from our countries. It seemed all five thousand people expected a gift, too, but we only made a few ceremonial pre-sentations — much to the chagrin of the crowd. The evening was ended by yet another meal, with the huge crowd pushing and shoving to get a glimpse of us eating. The next day we were ferried over to another island where twelve hundred refugees were living. A heavy spring runoff had washed their island out to sea. They barely had enough to eat and lived in makeshift housing. Here we distributed the clothes as well as sweets that the volunteers had bought.

We were guests in several other villages and at every stop we met a new set of dignitaries. At the end of our two days, exhausted and elated, we were escorted back to our ferry. Royalty could not have been treated better.

Safety and security

I arrived at my hotel at the same time as a woman who was from the United States. At the check-in counter, she asked many questions about hotel security and street safety. I could see that the answers she was receiving were not reassuring. In the next week, I caught a glimpse of her three times. The first two times, she looked worried and preoccupied. The third time, she was standing at the entrance to the hotel smiling. I asked what was making her so happy.

"Tonight I am going home. I can hardly wait!" she said.

"I gather you didn't like Calcutta?" I asked.

"No, I didn't," she exclaimed. I suggested we go for a coffee at the Blue Sky Café to talk about her adventures. To my astonishment she asked, "Where is that café?"

"About one hundred yards from here," I replied. "Everybody goes there." She made it clear that drinking coffee in an Indian restaurant to her meant sure death. I was flabbergasted by her reaction. She then told her story. She had taken a city bus tour the day after she had arrived. The other travellers had warned her over and over not to eat the food, and to be very careful. She had done exactly that for the past week — she had eaten only cheese and crackers, stayed in her room, read books, tried watching some TV. In one week she had not gone one hundred yards from the hotel, and had lived in fear. No wonder she was happy to go home.

My Way

As I sipped a chai (hot spiced tea and milk), I was watching a woman struggling with her suitcase. Since the suitcase's tiny wheels kept getting stuck in the potholes on the road, the woman tried the sidewalk, but the wheels got stuck in a crack and wouldn't budge. She tugged as hard as she could, and the strap broke. She kicked the suitcase, and sat down on the sidewalk sobbing. I offered to help, and she gratefully accepted.

We liberated the suitcase from the clutches of the sidewalk, then I took the strap to a cobbler. While the cobbler made repairs, the woman and I had tea. She said that she hailed from Italy and had come all the way to India to attend a conference on homeopathic medicine. She had a layperson's interest in this subject. The conference was in Goa, but there was an airline strike, and she refused to take a train or bus from Bombay to Goa. She had planned to purchase homeopathic remedies at the conference, but since she hadn't got to the conference she had come to Calcutta to acquire them. Her first problem was to find accommodation. She had tried everywhere, but everything was full. She asked if I would help her, and I agreed since I knew the area.

We went to seven hotels. Five had rooms available, but the woman rejected all five for one of these reasons: too expensive, too noisy, bed no good, peeling paint, windows too small. We were both exhausted from hauling her luggage around. After the seventh hotel, the woman announced out of the blue that she was going to find a Buddhist monastery to stay in. I was glad she had finally made a decision and wished her luck.

Two days later, she appeared at my hotel with her luggage and asked if I knew where College Street was. I said I did. She asked if I would take her. Reluctantly, I said I would. For four hours we walked up and down College Street looking for a shop with a blue awning. She had heard that the shop sold homeopathic remedies. Unable to find it, we quit searching. She told me that she was trying to get home early, since India had been "a real bust." Since her flight wasn't leaving for another four days, she had several feelers out with different travel agencies.

She left the luggage in my room and checked back with the travel agents. She arrived back at my hotel happily clutching a huge bag of remedies that she had bought on Park Street. She also had a ticket for a flight to Rome. It had cost her U.S. $1,000 — double the going rate. Had she waited four days, she could have flown on her original ticket. Later that night, when she left for the airport, the taxi fare used up every last bit of money she had, but she was satisfied. She had done things her way.

"No, you won't!"

I was travelling on Indian Airlines when we were told we were unable to proceed to our next stop. Our airplane was sitting on the tarmac when the communication came. A few minutes later, another announcement said that the passengers destined for the cancelled destination would be flown there later that day. About a dozen businessmen headed for the exit door at the front of the plane and told the cabin crew that the plane wasn't going anywhere.

A lot of shouting ensued, the passengers arguing that they been promised other things by Indian Airlines previously, and the promises hadn't been kept. The passengers wouldn't let the crew close the aircraft door. The shouting continued. After half an hour, the captain came out of the cockpit and tried to unravel the dilemma. The passengers refused to budge, however, and the captain retreated back to the cockpit. Ten minutes later, he reappeared and announced that we would land at an airport fifteen kilometres from our original destination, and buses would be waiting to transport the passengers. The protesters relented.

This experience served me well in India and in other countries. It always surprised me what could happen when I said, "No, you won't."

City Dump

My good friend, Lucy, wanted to visit the Calcutta city dump. I was delighted and surprised that someone besides myself was curious about the dump. We asked around for the location of the dump, but no one knew, nor did anyone understand our desire to investigate.

An MC (Missionaries of Charity) brother and I were bathing patients one morning when I shared my interest with him. He said he knew where the dump was, and if we were silly enough to want to go, he would arrange it. After work, Lucy and I recruited three more volunteers and the brother helped us hire a taxi for the trip. The first six taxis refused to take us, but the seventh agreed. We all piled into the cab and headed for the outskirts of the city. The driver refused to get too close to the dump, and made us get out a quarter of a mile away. We asked him to wait and said we would return in one hour.

We walked towards the tiny settlement next to the dump. It consisted of thirty dwellings, some sturdily built with bricks but most constructed from garbage. The houses were built around a pond filled with purple water, its consistency almost that of syrup. On the edge of the pond was a contraption belching out heavy black smoke. The contraption turned out be a still which produced lethal alcohol. The fire was fed using a pile of coconut shells, tires, shoes, plastic, leather, and anything else that

Calcutta city dump

was combustible. On the opposite side of the still was a pile of edibles like banana skins, orange peels, rotten tomatoes, potatoes, cabbages, and so on. The food products were fed into a barrel with tubes running out of it. At the end of the tubes were dirty glass bottles which caught the alcohol one drop at a time. I understood how consumers of this toxic product had been known to become blind.

We spent two hours in this small community, taking photographs, playing with the children, and trying to communicate with its citizens, none of whom spoke English. Then we spent another hour in the actual dump, where about a hundred people covered the fresh garbage like flies as they sorted through the refuse. We arrived back at our taxi two hours late, all of us so engrossed in our visit that we had forgotten the time. The driver was fuming. Even the extra money we gave him didn't improve his disposition. We were exhilarated after our stimulating trip to the dump, but he grumbled all the way back to the city.

Holi Festival

With India's many gods, there were always many festivals or pujas going on in Calcutta. Most were very noisy affairs. The Holi Festival was not particularly noisy, but it did catch me by surprise. For days prior to the festival, the shops sold huge quantities of coloured powder. On the day of the festival, as I walked down a narrow street lined with shops, a young fellow about twelve years old threw a handful of blue powder in my face. I chased after him, but he was too fast for me. I went back to my hotel, put on a clean shirt, and set out again.

This time, I had walked only about a block when someone dropped a balloon full of red liquid on me from the roof of a shop. Without success, I tried to find a way to get to the roof to punish the offender. Once again I changed clothes.

Unfortunately, I had to go down this street yet again. Liquid-filled balloons were being thrown everywhere. People were soaked with red, green, and blue. I proceeded very cautiously this time, and although many balloons were aimed at me, none hit the target. I only received a few spatters. Several blocks later, I was just congratulating myself about this when a group of young people spotted me and said I needed to get soaked and coloured. I asked them not to, and all but one backed off. This chap was very aggressive. To fend him off, I grabbed a rock and this infuriated him. We stood glaring at each other, each with our own weapon. Luckily, the situation was defused by a passing motorcycle police officer. He spoke no English, but with gestures tried to get me to drop the rock and the other chap to drop the water. My opponent was arguing with the officer about something, and the officer got off his motorcycle to deal with him. My assailant fled and I put the rock down.

Later, I compared notes with several of my fellow travellers. They had found this festival fun. I still felt grumpy. When I had a chance to think about it, I realized that I should have lightened up, and got into the spirit of the holiday. It would have been easier.

A Typical Restaurant

I was sitting in a plastic chair which used to be white, but was now various shades of gray. I leaned on the creamy arborite tabletop, and noticed amongst the numerous scratches the name "Harry." I tried to visualize what Harry would look like. Young? Old? Beard? I decided young, American, with a beard.

I switched my attention to the restaurant owner, who was sitting at a table parked halfway into the street. He was surrounded by bottles of mineral water and pop bottles in a rainbow of colours. He hadn't shaved for a few days and his shirt, which was bulging over his ample waist, was soiled. Exposing his stained teeth, he smiled and motioned to the parade of Westerners walking by, inviting them to come in. A cow sauntered past and the owner hugged the bottles to protect them from being knocked over by the beast. The cow sniffed the bottles and apparently decided that she wasn't interested in them. The owner relaxed, and the cow turned to mosey up the street. After she had taken a few steps, while she was taking aim with her tail at some pesky flies, she proceeded with one sweep to remove all the bottles from the table. Six bottles of pop shattered and all the others fell into a pile of cow manure. The owner called over the waiter to clean up the mess. The waiter washed the cow manure from the bottles and put them back on the table.

After watching this scene for some ten minutes, I was handed a greasy menu and a pencil, as well as a small piece of paper on which to write my order. Then the waiter picked up my piece of paper and took it to the kitchen. A few minutes later, he returned to complain about my hand writing. I told him verbally what I wanted, and he left for the kitchen again. After another ten minutes, he came back to inform me that they were out of chicken. Would fish be OK? I said it would. He brought my coffee with milk. I said that I didn't want milk. He said that I hadn't specified black — unless specified, coffee came with milk.

I apologized, and he brought black coffee, which tasted awful.

I enjoyed just sitting there watching everything. The street beggars were busy, and most Westerners picked up their pace to avoid them. More cows ambled by. Rock-and-roll music blared tinnily from a radio. Part of the label had been torn off the bottle of ketchup on my table, and the dried-up ketchup running down the side was covered with flies. Although it was January 30, the restaurant's Christmas decorations were still up, looking tattered. A photocopy of a poster was taped to the wall announcing yoga classes every Thursday night. From start to finish, the meal took one and a half hours. The entertainment was free.

Tour Guide in Calcutta

I was asked by a foreign tour group leader to spend three days with his group and give them the perspective of someone who spent a lot of time in Calcutta. When I met the group, I was confronted by a barrage of complaints: "It's too hot," "It's too dirty," and "At home we do it better." I spent three days biting my tongue and wondering why these people were in Calcutta. I made suggestions such as offering to buy them bottled water at the small shop down the street for 10 rupees rather than pay 54 rupees for bottled water at the hotel. They weren't interested. On one outing, a couple asked me to find them a taxi to get back to the hotel. I knew the fare to be about 10 rupees, and felt it would be reasonable for a Westerner to pay 15. The first taxi I hailed wanted 100 rupees, and I told him to go. The second asked for 50 rupees and again I told him we weren't interested. I also asked both drivers to use their meters (which would control the fare somewhat)

Typical bustee (slum) dwelling in Calcutta

In return for a few coins, this man allowed me to take his picture. He exists on donations which are placed by passers-by on the sheet held down by stones.

Calcutta sadhu (holy man) with receptacle for food or money donations

and they refused. I hailed a third cab. Before I even had a chance to negotiate, the tourist couple said, "We will pay whatever he asks." The cab driver just smiled. Later I found out that they had paid 200 rupees.

Near the end of the group's stay, we visited Kalighat, the place where I worked. A patient had been discharged and needed 78 rupees for train fare to return to his village. The group spent quite a bit of time talking to him. Since I knew that none of them was interested in saving money on water or cab fares, I suggested that someone pay his fare. No one volunteered.

The members of the tour group constantly bickered with each other. They were not a happy lot. After three days of living with them in luxury, I was very glad to escape back to my rat-infested room, cold showers and lumpy mattress. For many years, I had travelled like them, pampered and complaining. Sure, I still complained sometimes, but it didn't last. Most of the time I was very happy to be where I was, and had learned to be grateful even for the lumpy mattress.

Health

How to stay healthy in India? I worried about that a lot when I first started going to Calcutta. There was excrement everywhere — from humans, sacred cows, and pets. Add to that the poor air quality. I had been to Los Angeles, California, where the pollution count was considered high at 30 or 40, but in Calcutta, the count could be as high as 250. To top it all off, I was working with dying people.

Over time, I began to believe that the best way to stay healthy in India was attitude. I became convinced that most health problems while travelling in India were caused by excessive concern about health. Some newcomers to India could be recognized by their worried looks and by their behaviour in restaurants. They would clean the silverware, pop pills, add drops to bottled drinking water, and try to draw people's attention to a mouse or rat. In my experience, it was wise to be cautious, but to be preoccupied about health only created more problems. My prescription became: "Don't Worry." I did get sick in India, but the time I spent being ill was relatively short. Whenever I got dysentery, for example, I learned to take a stool specimen for analysis, then take the results to a pharmacy for the appropriate remedy. In four to seven days my system would be restored to normal.

One time, I had felt sharp pain in my stomach for several weeks. When the pain spread to my jaw, I became a little concerned, since at work two patients had just died from lockjaw. I decided to ignore the pain and go to a movie. Sitting behind me were my neighbours, George and Angie. They noticed that I was in discomfort. After some questioning, Angie, who was a nurse, insisted I go to the hospital. I vigorously protested, but after a while agreed. To make sure that I did go, they escorted me. At the hospital the doctor took several tests, and found the only abnormality was high blood pressure. He suggested I be hospitalized. Angie said that she would watch me that evening and it would not be necessary to retain me. The doctor was concerned that I might be suffering from stress and suggested that I be careful. I told him that I had absolutely no stress.

The next day at work, I spoke with our doctor. After taking my blood pressure, he also was concerned about stress and sent me to get a series of blood tests. Two doctors were concerned that I had too much stress and each time I was denying that there was a problem. I decided to monitor a typical day, and prove that no stress existed. Getting sick was for the weak, not for me!

My job at work was coordinator of volunteers. The day that I decided to monitor my day's activities, I arrived, as was my custom, before any other volunteers. The night crew of paid employees had assembled the dead bodies and wrapped them in white sheets (or shrouds), and placed them near the entrance to await pick-up by the ambulance. Since nothing urgent was happening, I decided to check the identity of the bodies. I loosened the safety pin on the first shroud to uncover the head. Immediately, a pain hit my gut as inwardly I screamed, Oh no! Not Ranjat! He was only eighteen and had been the definite favourite of all the volunteers. Always cheerful and smiling, his face radiated love, and he was passionate about cuddles. Why did he have to die? I asked myself. He was so young and so happy. Why him? My gut wrenched with pain. Maybe it was trying to tell me I was affected by the work?

Further down the ward, another body was lying on a stretcher. I unpinned the shroud to check on its identity. This one was less surprising, but still hit that spot in my gut. For two years, Mr. Bannergee had been in bed forty-three. He too had been a favourite with me. He couldn't talk, but we established a special communication that we both understood. We had formed a special bond, and I no longer could look forward to spending time with this sweet man. I felt the loss much more than I would have predicted. Throughout the day, I found myself reacting to the day's events with impatience and intolerance. By the end of the day, I realized that stress was probably a factor in my high blood pressure, and I had better start taking better care of myself. For one thing, I needed to reduce my attachments to the patients and diminish my sense of self-importance.

When the results of my blood tests came back, they indicated high blood sugar, high cholesterol, and an unknown stomach infection likely caused by my over-confidence in the water supply. My prolonged stomach discomfort could have been avoided by being a bit more cautious. My inspiration came from the sisters I worked with. They had all been exposed to patients with tuberculosis, leprosy and AIDS. To the best of my knowledge, none of the sisters ever contracted any of these diseases. When I have a thirst for water in India, I try to take reasonable precautions and use bottled water. When it comes to satisfying my thirst for enjoying life and exploring a new culture, I hope to stay healthy, but if not, I will enjoy that journey also. For enjoying the journey is my thirst.

~

Epilogue

I am sitting at my computer thinking how fortunate I am. I have a magnificent view from my thirtieth-floor apartment right in the heart of Vancouver. I have a cottage on an island. Yet I feel a strong urge to strap on my

Michael de Jong, 1995

backpack and head for the road. Some of my well-meaning friends suggest that I am just restless. Perhaps that is true. I do know that I fear staying here too long — my life might become too mechanical and I might revert back to my robot existence. In the last seven years, I went from barely existing to fullness, from caring only for myself to feeling compassion for others. I long for experiences that are worthwhile, rewarding . . . and exciting. What's next? Perhaps Africa?

ORDER FORM

I Thirst

Seven Trips to India

Also available from your local bookstore.

CANADIAN FUNDS		U.S. FUNDS	
____ Copies @ $16.95	$_____	____ Copies @ $14.95	$_____
GST (7%)	$_____		
Shipping (1st book)	$ 4.00	Shipping (1st book)	$ 2.50
Add $2 for each		Add $1.50 for each	
additional book	$_____	additional book	$_____
Total enclosed	$_____	Total enclosed	$_____

Make cheque or money order payable to:

Michael de Jong

Name _____

Address _____

City, Province/State_____

Postal/Zip Code_____

Phone (work) _____ (home) _____

FOCUS PRESS

Focus Press

P.O. Box 47022, Denman Place P.O.
Vancouver, BC Canada V6G 3E1

Michael de Jong is available for speaking engagements.
For information, call (604) 816-8401.

email: IThirst@bc.sympatico.ca

Thank you for your order!